WRECKING THE ARMOURED TRAIN AT KRAAIPAN.

By permission of "The Daily Graphic."

MAFEKING

A

Diary of the Siege

BY

MAJOR F. D. BAILLIE

LATE IVTH (Q. O.) HUSSARS

By permission of " The Daily Graphic."
SIGNALLING FROM AN ARMOURED TRAIN.

WITH NUMEROUS ILLUSTRATIONS

The Naval & Military Press Ltd

in association with

The National Army Museum, London

Published jointly by

The Naval & Military Press Ltd

Unit 10 Ridgewood Industrial Park,
Uckfield, East Sussex,
TN22 5QE England

Tel: +44 (0) 1825 749494
Fax: +44 (0) 1825 765701

www.naval-military-press.com
www.military-genealogy.com
www.militarymaproom.com

and

The National Army Museum, London

www.national-army-museum.ac.uk

Prefatory Note

I must crave the indulgence of the public for producing a more or less rough form of diary in the form of a book, and it is only the interest which they have manifested in Mafeking which has induced me to do so. To the proprietor of *The Morning Post* I am indebted for his kindness in allowing me to re-publish the diary in book form. To the proprietors of *The Daily Graphic* I am indeed grateful for the sketches with which they have allowed me to supplement my diary. Such as it is, I dedicate it to all members of my dear old regiment, past and present. Four of us were serving there : myself, and

Private Brierly, B squadron, now B. S. A. P., Private Williams and Private Lambart, D squadron (the former now sergeant), Protectorate Regiment, while the adjutant of the I. L. H. portion of the relieving force was Captain Barnes, also B squadron. These are only matters of regimental interest, but as the publication is dedicated to the regiment, I feel justified in giving these details.

F. D. BAILLIE, Major,
late 4th Queen's Own Hussars.

The Siege of Mafeking

" WAR declared to-night, October 10th, 1899,
by old Kruger. So much the better, this
intolerable waiting is over." This I find is the
entry in my diary for that date, but little did
I know we were about to commence the
" Siege of Mafeking "—a much more intolerable wait, with the additional pleasure of
being fired at without the chance of returning
it with effect.

Till you have experienced it no one (at
least I hadn't) has any idea how trying it is
to exist without news of the outside world.

On October 11th nothing happened. On
the 12th, the Protectorate Regiment under
Colonel Hore took up a position on the
eastern heights, which overlook the town

and waited attack. The Boers, however, did not arrive.

In the meantime the town defences under Colonel Vyvyan and Major Panzera were progressing apace. We had only quite recently been enabled to do anything in that direction, owing to the repressive policy of the Bond Ministry. Therefore the defences at this time consisted merely of a few breastworks, wagons drawn across the ends of roads leading on to the market square, and a few strands of barbed wire fastened up on these points.

October 13th, 1899. In the morning the same programme ; the Boers reported to the south and also to the north. Whilst lying on the heights—if they can be so called—we saw a magnificent sight. For safety two trucks of dynamite were being run up to a northern siding clear of the town. About eight miles out the Boers commenced firing. The engine-driver uncoupled his trucks and ran his engine back towards the town. The Boers closed in and continued firing, thinking it was the armoured train. Result—a terrific explosion, a column of smoke shooting up into the air and mushrooming out until it became a vast cloud in the clear blue sky. In the afternoon I went out in the armoured train to inspect the damage, but they had pulled up the line short of the spot. We opened with a Maxim on the body of Boers engaged in inspecting the hole and bagged a couple. The remainder galloped in the utmost confusion towards their laager.

The armoured train had previously been out in the morning due south and bagged one, and went out again in the same direction on its return, under Captain Williams, and secured another.

October 14th, 1899. The fight to-day may be summarized thus: Boers firing on the picquets; Boer retirement harassed by the armoured train, which was eventually supported by one squadron, which engaged the retreating Boers heavily. The Boers tried to cut them off, but the arrival of another squadron and a seven-pounder settled the matter. Their attack was repelled with great loss, and we retired to our lines.

Whilst we were at breakfast firing was heard in the direction of the cemetery to the

north of the town, and shortly afterwards
increased in volume ; then came the bark of
the Maxim, the boom of heavy guns and the
increasing rattle of musketry. D squadron
of the Protectorate Regiment was ordered out
to support the armoured train. We waited
on the Market Square knowing nothing,
hearing only the heavy fire.

What had transpired was this : a squadron
of the Protectorate Regiment commanded by
Lord Charles Bentinck had furnished a strong
patrol to discover the whereabouts of the
Boers. He happened to come upon them about
four miles out. They promptly pursued and
tried to cut him off. The Corporal with his
right flank patrol galloped on to the armoured
train, and on his own initiative directed it to
move out in support. The Boers were driven
back, hotly engaged by the armoured train,
in charge of Captain Williams, British South
Africa Police, a train which was constructed
and conducted by Lieutenant More, Railway
Volunteers. The train drove their artillery
from two positions ; their shells burst all
round, under and over the train, and, strange
to say, only two men were slightly scratched.

THE CREW OF H.M.S. "FIREFLY." *By permission of "The Daily Graphic."*

At that period Captain Fitzclarence arrived, and engaged the Boers who were withdrawing, firing at the armoured train, towards their own laager. To explain the situation now, I must describe the field of battle. The railway runs due north and south of Mafeking. The Boers' laager about eight miles N.N.E. of the town. The train had driven the enemy about five miles and a half back from the town, therefore by this divergence, when Captain Fitzclarence came into action he had perforce lost the effective support of the train, and the squadron fought on its own account. It numbered about seventy men : it faced about five or six hundred. Two orderlies were sent to Captain Fitzclarence and the armoured train to tell them to fall back, one on a bicycle who was captured, and the other on horseback.

Now to show the advantage of khaki as a fighting colour on the well-bleached Veldt. The horseman rode up to the Boers and was fired upon. He then galloped along the front of, and through and along the rear of our own men without seeing a man, delivered his message to the armoured train, and returned to seek his invisible friends unsuccessfully. His horse was shot, and he returned to Mafeking on an engine. In at least two instances he was within thirty yards of his own men and could not see them. The dark clothing of the Boers is, however, more conspicuous, but with smokeless powder and khaki the firing line even at short ranges is invisible as a target.

To return to the actual fight. The Boers pelted by a well-directed fire returned a wild and ineffectual one. The incidents of the fight commenced. Two cousins, Corporals Walshe and Parland, Irishmen, and men of means who had joined not for pay but for patriotism, quickly fell, both shot through the head by the same Dutchman, who was ensconced in a tree, but unfortunately for himself he let fall a piece of paper which caught the quick eye of Private Wormald, who promptly picked him off like a rook. Several other Dutchmen in like positions met the same fate. This treatment did not appeal to the Boer, who came out to shoot and not to be shot at, and so he made his usual move to work round and cut off the squadron from their base.

At the distance the squadron was from the line (over three quarters of a mile), and at the angle it was to the line, in addition to the difficulty with smokeless powder of telling friend from foe, it was impossible for the armoured train to act. Previous to this they had been supported by a troop of A squadron under Lieutenant Brady who was wounded on coming into action. The situation was distinctly serious, their flank was nearly turned, and the Boers had almost interposed themselves between the squadron and Mafeking ; at this critical juncture Lord Charles Bentinck and two more troops with a seven-pound gun arrived within striking distance. Two rounds of shrapnel and the Boers commenced retiring. When their retirement was assured D squadron withdrew, placing their wounded in the armoured train. The fight was over.

Surgeon-Major Anderson, who had had his horse shot, attended to the wounded throughout the fight in the firing line. Our losses were two killed, twelve wounded, two of whom subsequently died. Four horses killed, twelve wounded. Boer losses reported eighty killed, about twice that number wounded.

2

Too much credit cannot be given to
Captain Fitzclarence and Lord Charles
Bentinck for the coolness and gallantry
with which they handled their men, or to the
men for the way they responded, and what
is said of them applies in the same degree
to Captain Williams and the men of the
British South Africa Police and Railway
Volunteers engaged. The Boers had fought
in the scrubb, in vastly superior numbers
and had been thoroughly beaten.

The strain on Colonel Baden-Powell and
the headquarter staff must indeed have been
great. For four hours they were anxiously
waiting, reports were not favourable, and they
knew that a disaster to a small force engaged
risked the whole defence as there was literally
not another man to send to their support.
Indeed one squadron engaged was actually a
part of the defence of the northern portion of
the town. On the return of the wounded a train
with a relief party under Major Baillie with
Father Ogle, and Mr. Peart, Wesleyan
minister, went to recover the bodies, and if
necessary to render assistance to any wounded
Boers who might have been left in the

retreat. The train stopped near the scene
of the action and the party with stretchers,
preceded by a large Red Cross flag,
moved towards the spot. They were fired on
about half a mile before they reached it, and
as the firing increased it was decided to
retire as the men were known to be dead,
and all the wounded were brought in.

This they did quietly, the Boers in the
meantime were working round to the line to
cut them off from the train. The train returned
to Mafeking, and on a report being made to
Colonel Baden-Powell he addressed a letter
of remonstrance to General Cronje.

15th, Sunday. Landau and pair, with
huge Red Cross flag, arrived containing Dr.
Pirow, Cronje's doctor, who came to lunch.
He explained that the firing on the Red Cross
was a mistake, as the Boers thought that the
train was the armoured train returning, and
gave us news of Lieutenant Nesbitt and our
prisoners of the armoured train which has been
captured at Kraaipan. He took whisky and
beer back with him for Cronje. Sunday is
a tacit truce with both parties, and no fighting
goes on. I suppose we are the only two

2 *

Nations who would observe it. The ambulance
went out and fetched in the dead. They
were buried by moonlight by Father Ogle,
a most impressive ceremony. The Father
said a few words to the effect that it was
a righteous war, and that the Sisters were
praying for us.

16th, Monday. The Boers brought up two
twelve-pounders to a long-range position
N.-E. of the town and commenced bombarding. They drove in our picquet at the head
of the waterworks and occupied the trench.
They directed their fire mainly on the town
and station, consequently did most damage in
the convent, which was flying the Red Cross
and was fitted up as a hospital. The shells
that missed the convent struck the centre
of the town, but did little harm. The shells
that missed the station pitched round the
B. S. A. P. fort, which was occupied by
Colonel Hore and a squadron of the Protectorate Regiment. This they continued
all day. Casualties *nil*. Our seven-pounders
out-ranged. No reply made to their fire.

The Boers had thus occupied the head of
the waterworks and cut off our water supply.

The headquarter staff had made provision for this, and under Major Hepworth's supervision had had all wells cleaned out and Sir Charles Warren's old well reopened. We thus have an abundance of water.

Towards mid-day a flag of truce, borne by a renegade English Colonial, rode towards our lines. This was unfortunate. They had not detected the armoured train, and the skirmishing line of the Boers and their artillery was just coming within deadly Maxim range. They rode straight on to the armoured train, and of course the trap was disclosed. It was a message from Cronje, who sent in to demand surrender to avoid further bloodshed. Baden-Powell answered, " Certainly, but when will bloodshed begin ? " and pointed out that they were again firing on the Red Cross flag.

Two of our wounded, both corporals, died to-day. The town is practically surrounded.

17th, 18th, and 19th. Nothing happened. Investment completed. Boers estimated six thousand men, undoubtedly correct.

20th. Boers cut off some cattle which had strayed out too far.

21st. In addition to the main railway

line, a temporary line had been laid down in an easterly direction towards the race course, and north of the town extending about a mile and a half. The armoured train now patrolled this line ; painted green and covered with bushes, it was indistinguishable from the scrub surrounding it. I slept in the armoured train at the rail-head. In the early morning Captain Williams commenced firing on the Boers at the head of the waterworks as they came out of their trench to make their coffee, with two Maxims. I fear they got their coffee rather late, and that some even did not get it at all. This went on with fitful replies for two or three hours, and then firing in that quarter ceased.

On the western front in the afternoon the Boers looted some cattle which had strayed, and from this date sniping commenced, pretty generally all round on both sides.

22nd, Sunday. Band and calls on various outlying forts, hospitals, &c. All church services were held.

And now to endeavour to describe the town and defences of Mafeking. Mafeking is situated on a rise about three hundred

FIRING FROM AN ARMOURED TRAIN.

By permission of "The Daily Graphic."

yards north of the Molopo river, which flows from east to west. It is about three-quarters of a mile square. The railroad runs to the west of the town, and practically speaking, due north and south, but immediately south where it crosses the Molopo by an iron bridge it inclines rather westward for a distance of two or three miles. The railway embankment north and south of the river thus furnishes cover from the east and south-east heights on the southern bank of the Molopo. To the west again of the railway, and nearly butting it half a mile south of the Molopo, is the native stadt, lying on both sides of the river, and on the northern bank, commencing about half a mile from the railway, then running in a north-westerly direction for about a mile and a half, and ends about a mile and three-quarters west of the railway. The ground in front of the northern end is slightly higher than the stadt and soon commences to sink away from it, affording good cover to an enemy moving on that side. Near the railway the ground slopes gradually down for a considerable distance to the river. The country round

Mafeking to the west, north and east, is flat, but across the Molopo to the south and south-east it commands the town. The ground to the west of the stadt commands the stadt.

Situated two thousand yards south, and slightly east of the centre of the town, is an old fort of Sir Charles Warren's—Cannon Kopje. This is the key of the position. It is an old circular stone fort, and only by dint of extraordinary exertion had it been possible to bring it by this time up in any degree to a state of efficiency enough to enable it to resist even old ordinary seven-pounder guns. It has an interior diameter of approximately twenty-five yards. The native location occupied by half-breeds lies directly between Cannon Kopje and the town on the southern bank of the river. Following the course of the river eastward about twelve hundred yards from the town, and on the northern bank extend the brickfields (eventually occupied by both parties), while in the same direction, and about three miles and a half from Mafeking on a ridge, is MacMullan's farm (subsequently the Boer headquarters). To return to the

town—at the north-eastern corner is the
convent. Due east of that is the grand stand
about a mile away, while N.N.E. from the
convent, and a mile and a half away, is the
base of the waterworks, which extend to
a trench at their head in the same direction
for nearly a mile.

Thus we have the railway station the
north-west corner, the convent the north-east
corner, Ellis's house the south-east corner,
and the south-west corner the pound ; while
in a line from the south-west corner of the
town and the northern portion of the stadt,
the B. S. A. P. barracks and fort lie about
midway. With the exception of a strip of
scrub about a mile wide to the north and east
of the convent the country all round is almost
bare.

The town is composed of one-storey houses
built of soft bricks and roofed with corrugated
iron, the only exception being the convent of
two storeys and the station, which is not yet
complete. The native stadt consists of Kaffir
huts. The B. S. A. P. fort is a duplicate
of Cannon Kopje, thus the outline of the
defences of Mafeking is, roughly speaking,

an obtuse angled triangle, of which the apex is Cannon Kopje, while the other two angles are the northern end of the native stadt and the convent. The population in time of peace is, Mafeking two thousand whites, the native stadt four to five thousand, location five hundred. At the present moment fifteen hundred whites approximately, native stadt seven thousand owing to native refugees, location five hundred.

The perimeter of the defences was between five and six miles. Commencing with the convent, and working westward at the outset, the defences were as follows :—The railway line and armoured train protected the north-west front, then nearer to the railway came Fort Victoria, occupied by Railway Volunteers; and in the arc of a circle extending to the north end of the stadt trenches occupied by the Protectorate Regiment at night. These were gradually turned into forts. The women's laager was established on the edge of the stadt near the B. S. A. P. officers' quarters, and a refugee camp in the hollow north of the stadt, the northern end of which was held by Captain Vernon and

C squadron Protectorate Regiment, while B squadron, under Captain Marsh, and the natives, held the stadt itself—the whole under Major Godley, who commanded the western outposts. The town was garrisoned by the Cape Police under Captains Brown and Marsh; these and the Railway Volunteers being under Colonel Vyvyan, while Cannon Kopje was entrusted to Colonel Walford and the B. S. A. P. Colonel Baden-Powell retained one squadron of the Protectorate Regiment as reserve under his own immediate control. These arrangements were subsequently much augmented. After the convent had been practically demolished by shell fire and the railway line all round the town pulled up or mined during the close investment by the Boers, the small work was erected at the convent corner, garrisoned by the Cape Police and a Maxim, under Lieutenant Murray, who was also put in charge of the armoured train, which had, however, been withdrawn to the railway station out of harm's way. The Railway Volunteers garrisoned the cemetery, and had an advanced trench about eight hundred yards to the front and

immediately to the right of the line. To the
westward came Fort Cardigan, and then again
Fort Miller. In the south-west was Major
Godley's fort, at the north of the native
stadt, with an advance fort—Fort Ayr—
crowning the down to the northern end of the
stadt. Although this was rather detached,
it commanded a view and fire for a great distance to the south of the northern portion of
the stadt, and here the Cape Police were entrenched with the Maxim. Five hundred yards
to the west front of Captain Marsh's post lay
Limestone fort, commanding the valley, on
the other side of which lay the Boer laager
and entrenchments. At the south-western
corner, and on the edge of the stadt Captain
Marsh's fort was situated. The whole of the
edge of the stadt was furnished with loop-
holes and trenches, and garrisoned by the
native inhabitants. By the railway were
situated two armoured trucks with a Nordenfeldt. Cannon Kopje, with two Maxims and
a seven-pounder, lay to the south-east. And
now to the immediate defence of the town.
At the south-western corner is the pound,
garrisoned by Cape Police, under Captain

Marsh ; then eastwards Early's fort, Dixon's redan, Dall's fort, Ellis's corner, with Maxim and Cape Police, under Captain Brown. On the eastern front, Ellitson's kraal, Musson's fort, De Kock's fort, with Maxim, recreation ground fort, and so back to the convent, on the left of which lies the hospital fort—all these, unless otherwise mentioned, garrisoned by Town Guard. These so-called forts are garrisoned with from fifteen to forty men, and furnished with head cover and bomb proofs against artillery. Bomb proofs have been constructed everywhere, traverses erected at the end of streets, trenches giving cover leading from every portion of the town and defences ; and it is possible to walk round the town without being exposed to aimed fire. The trenches are constructed with a view to being manned in case of need. Telephones are established in all the head-quarter bomb proofs of outlying forts, and are connected with the headquarter bomb proof, thus securing instant communication and avoiding the chance of orderlies being sniped, which would assuredly otherwise be the case. These defences were all improvised on the spot—every conceivable sort of material being utilized therein.

23rd, Monday. Bombardment threatened, so commenced by forestalling it. Two guns under Captain Williams, B. S. A. P., and Lieutenant Murchison, Protectorate Regiment, started at 3 a.m., to take up a position at our end of the waterworks and the rail head temporary line, respectively, with orders not to fire unless fired on. I rode out with them and saw as pretty an artillery duel in miniature as one would wish to see. We waited patiently, Lieutenant Murchison laid his gun on the enemy's seven-pounder, which we could distinctly see in their trenches at the head of the waterworks. We were under cover from view. At last a puff of smoke came from their gun, and before it was well clear of the muzzle ours had answered, and that gun was out of action for a considerable period. In the meantime, both of our guns were playing gaily on their trenches and remaining gun. This went on intermittently till mid-day, and then both their guns ceased fire altogether. We then returned, and since heard that their guns were rendered useless for some time. On the south-western portion of the defences a similar seven-pounder fight was going on, and the Boers then fired their twelve-pounder high velocity gun a few times. Their ninety-four-pounder Creechy (an abbreviation for Marguerite) or, as the men call her, Creaky, has arrived and taken up a position at Jack-all Tree, 3400 yards S.S.W. of Cannon Kopje, accompanied by some field guns.

24th. Creaky commenced her ministrations by firing about forty shells and damaged property but hurt no one. The convent of course was hit, and the twelve-pounders also joined in the fire. Marvellous escapes reported all round.

25th. Creaky began in real earnest, and also seven-pounders, twelve-pounders, Maxims, and all. They fired about four hundred shells, mostly in the direction of the convent hospital, trying, I fancy, to hit the station. I was in the trenches in the recreation ground. The convent was struck several times. Their shell fire seemed very noisy, but its effect was more moral than physical, as casualties therefrom were few ; the musketry fire, however, did more damage. The advance party down the Malmani road had a man hit badly (since dead), young Kelly, Protectorate Regiment, and when a party went out to fetch him, though obviously wounded, they were exposed to a hail of bullets—for at least half a mile. I saw the lad in the hospital, and his only anxiety was to get out and have another go at them. At the same time on the other flank the Boers made an attack on the native staff, hoping on the assurance of the Baralongs to obtain a footing there; and then when they had got us thoroughly engaged on the south-western face, their real attack was to have been made from the north. The Baralongs, however, supplemented by two squadrons of ours, greeted them with a heavy fire, killing many. Consequently that attack on our face never came off.

27th. Shelling continued, and now, having beaten the enemy in the field, Colonel Baden-Powell resolved to give them a taste of cold steel, accordingly, at 8 p.m. D squadron, fifty-three strong, paraded under Captain Fitzclarence, with two parties of the Cape Police in support. It was a fine dark night, and the squadron moved off with injunctions only to use the bayonet. The two parties of Cape Police moved towards the brickfields, one considerably further east than the other to enfilade the rear of the Boer trenches. The object of the attack was some trenches of Commandant Louw's on our side of the race-course and to the north of the Malmani road (which runs due east of the town to Malmani). It was a still night, and lying waiting one could hear the order to charge, and then the din began. The first trench was carried with a rush ; the Boers lying under tarpaulins did not hear the advance till they were almost on them. Sword and bayonet did their work well, and with the flanking parties firing on the rear trench, and the Boers commencing a heavy fire in all directions and from all quarters, things for a time were very lively indeed. It was estimated that six hundred Boers were in laager, so after giving them a thorough dose of the bayonet, the signal to retire was given by a loud whistle, and carried out in the same cool and orderly manner as the advance. In the meantime a furious fire was being maintained by the Boers all round ;

3 *

the volleys from the Cape Police completed
their confusion, and they kept on firing even
after the wounded had been dressed and
placed in hospital. Something frightened
them again about 2 a.m., and they recommenced their fusilade at nothing and continued
it for about an hour. Our losses were six
killed, eleven wounded and two prisoners,
including Captain Fitzclarence and Lieutenant
Swinburne slightly wounded. We subsequently heard that the Boers lost one hundred
—forty killed by the bayonet, and sixty whom
they had probably shot themselves in the
hideous confusion that reigned in their camp.
Captain Fitzclarence used his sword with good
effect. The Cape Police, who were under
Lieutenant Murray, lost none. The attacking
squadron did not fire a shot, but in the rush
to the second trench the occupants probably
shot their own men in the dark at close range.
This story later shows the terror the Boers here
have of cold steel. Our snipers were now close
to the enemy's trench, and one of the Boers,
probably an artilleryman, waved his sword
over the top, whereupon one of his comrades
was overheard to shout, " For God's sake do

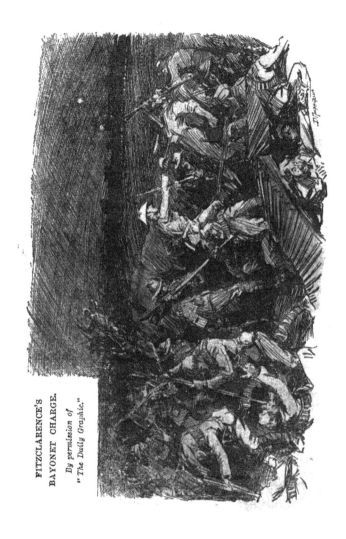

FITZCLARENCE'S
BAYONET CHARGE.

*By permission of
"The Daily Graphic."*

not do that, or they will come with their bayonets."

What I said about coolness and gallantry in the first fight applies in even a greater degree to this encounter. The men were admirably led and did splendidly. Our success so far was marked. The Boers had been kept at a respectful distance from the town. They never felt safe at night; they had been beaten at their own game in the open, and we practically disregarded their vaunted artillery, on which they had pinned their faith to reduce the town. Daily the situation became more a question of endurance.

28th. Ambulance, under a flag of truce, fetched in our dead. Boers very surly. The dead were buried that night. Shell-fire and sniping continued; little harm done.

29th, Sunday. Band, &c.

30th. Transferred my residence to the western portion to watch the Boers moving to and fro on our western front, about two miles out, sniping going on both sides all round. Desultory shell fire.

31st. Enemy's force occupied a position on the south-eastern heights and from Jackall

Tree three thousand four hundred yards
S.S.W. of Cannon Kopje, where they had
erected earthworks, their artillery pushed
forward to within two thousand yards, and
opened a heavy fire on the kopje, commencing
at 4.40 a.m., under cover of which their infantry attack was pushed from the south-east
to within three hundred yards of the kopje,
but was repelled by the B. S. A. P., fifty-seven
strong, with two Maxims and a seven-pounder
under Colonel Walford. They attacked with
great resolution, but our fire was held till they
came within good range, and then after sus-
taining it for some time they broke and fled.
Their ambulances came to pick up the dead and,
under their cover, many who had been playing " possum " got up and ran for their lives.
Our losses were six killed, including Captain
the Hon. D. H. Marsham and Captain Pechell,
K.R.R., and two sergeant-majors, five wounded
severely. I may perhaps be permitted to
say a few words about personal friends. It
seemed as if it could not be true. In Captain
Marsham's case, well known as he was to the
Boers, and popular as he was on both sides of
the border, the enemy will regret his death

almost as deeply as his comrades here did.
Captain Pechell had a brother serving here as
a private in the Protectorate, who has since
got his commission in that regiment; an
additional sympathy must be felt for his
family and regiment, as almost at the same
time his brother in the same regiment was
killed in a Natal fight. I only voice the one
feeling here of personal sorrow for their loss
and sympathy with their relations.

The Boers were well thrashed, and my previous description of Cannon Kopje will enable
readers to grasp what a thoroughly gallant
fight it was. The Boers must have lost very
heavily. Later in the day they attacked the
southern end of the native stadt, in a half-
hearted manner, but it was not pushed home,
and were easily driven off. Both these fights
were easily visible across the valley, with the
exception of the commencement of the Boer
infantry advance, which one could only gather
from the continuous musketry fire. This
night we buried the dead, all the available
officers in the garrison attending.

November 1st. The enemy shelled Cannon
Kopje again, and galloped up from the south

within about a mile, dismounted, and made a show of attack, but were driven away. Shell fire and sniping.

2nd. Desultory shell fire and lots of sniping at horses watering, five horses wounded. At about 10 p.m. Lieutenant Murchison shot Mr. Parslow, *Daily Chronicle* representative, but as the matter is still *sub judice*, comments or opinions are undesirable.

3rd. Heavy shelling and sniping. The Boers having occupied a position in the brick-fields, Captain Goodyear and the Cape Boys attacked them and turned them out, during which Captain Goodyear was unfortunately severely wounded in the leg.

Inquest this morning returned a verdict of wilful murder against Lieutenant Murchison, who will be tried by Field General Court Martial. Mr. Parslow's funeral took place to-night, attended by the staff and many others; the other correspondents and myself carried the coffin to the grave.

4th. Heavy shelling and sniping all round, eight horses shot. The Boers having experienced the delights of the dynamite explosion, now determine to repay us in our own coin.

Loading a truck with dynamite, they brought it up to the top of the incline on the railway, which runs from the north down to Mafeking Station, meaning to run it into the station and explode it in the town. In this amiable intention they were foiled, as either owing to the rustiness or roughness of the line, which had not been used for three weeks, to the defective fuse, or some other unexplained cause, it blew up a mile and a half out of town, and I trust assisted a few of them to the other world. The curious part of the explosion was that everyone insisted that a shell had burst exactly over the spot he happened to be in, and it was not until next day that the occurrence was explained.

5th. Sunday. Band, and celebrated Guy Fawkes day with fireworks, first warning the enemy not to be alarmed.

6th. A smart bit of work on the part of the Boers. Their big gun opened fire at 4.30 a.m., and after firing one shot they took her round to the south-eastern heights, where they had erected a work for her, and fired again within twelve hours; by the remote road they preferred, it must have been more

than four miles ; two field guns and a large
escort accompanied her.

7th.   Rumours were rife as to the intended
attack on the native stadt this morning, but
this pleasant attention was anticipated.   At
3 a.m. Major Godley paraded with Captain
Vernon's squadron, Protectorate Regiment
and mounted Bechuanaland Rifles under
Captain Cowan, with two seven-pounders and
the Hotchkiss gun, under Lieutenant Daniel,
B. S. A. P., Captain Marsh's Squadron P. R.,
being held in readiness to support, if necessary,
from the southern portion of the stadt.   And
here it must be explained that due west
the Boers had established a laager with about
two hundred and fifty men, two twelve-
pounders and a diabolical one-pound Maxim
in entrenchments, and daily shelled the stadt
and western defences, and that it was from
this quarter that the attack was expected.
However, Major Godley took up a position
within good range of the laager, and as day
broke the Boers were roused by the seven-
pounders and the Hotchkiss, supplemented by
long range volleys.   The Boers broke to ward
Cronje's large laager, about three or four

miles south-west of the stadt. I was watching operations from the top of the B. S. A. P. fort, and the whole fight was clearly discernible in its earlier stages, an admirable example of Boer tactics, as their advance to

RELICS.

their attacking position was across our western front, though at safe distance from rifle fire. Within ten minutes of the commencement of fire knots of Boers came galloping from the large laager, in tens, twenties, twos and threes, anyhow, in fact, and about half way they met

the Boers who were retreating, who then
rallied and returned with them to the attack.
They swept over the ridge towards the north,
and as they drew nearer were assailed by long
range volleys from Captain Marsh, and then
the fight began.   There could not have been
less than five hundred, personally I fancy
eight.   Their guns were in full swing and
firing wildly fortunately, for the majority of
the shells burst by the women's laager and
the fort, which did not seem logical, as we
were not hurting them.   Their one-pound
Maxim, however, was putting in good work.
The object of the sortie had been attained in
drawing the attack where we wanted it, and
a gradual and slow retirement on the works
commenced.   Then, unfortunately, one of
our guns was temporarily disabled, but under
a very heavy fire was righted without any
casualty, which was miraculous, as the one-
pounder had got the range and put shells
around it all the time, shooting off the heel
of a man's boot and bursting all around and
among the men and horses.   However, all
got under cover all right.   Captain Vernon
handled his men coolly and well, and retiring

by alternate troops they kept the enemy at
bay. The fire was very heavy, and but that the
majority of the Boer firing was wild, we
should have lost heavily. Major Godley was
shot through the hat, slightly wounded in the
hand, and his horse shot. The Bechuanaland
Rifles at their baptism of fire behaved steadily
and well, and Captain Cowan was well justified
at his pride in his men. The Boers attacked
the entrenchments, advancing to within six
hundred yards of them, but were beaten off
with loss. Working round to the northern
flank, however, they managed to account for
eleven horses and two men in about as many
seconds, but the undesirable attention of the
stationary Maxim convinced them that their
presence was no longer necessary. It was
very hot whilst it lasted, and then to the
looker-on came the welcome sight of first one,
then twos and threes, then larger bodies, canter-
ing off in the direction from which they had
come, and then, the most welcome sight of all,
three large wagons flying the Red Cross flag
coming to pick up their casualties, showing
that their loss must have been heavy. Our
loss, six men wounded, six horses killed, nine

wounded, and many cattle and donkeys in the vicinity of the forts killed and wounded.

8th. Sniping and shelling and a new earthwork being constructed by the Boers three thousand yards due north of the B. S. A. P. fort, called Game Tree fort.

9th. The cheering news from Natal of three British victories has arrived, great excitement prevails, and naturally—it is our first news for nearly a month. Shelling and sniping of course goes on, and one shell burst in Colonel Walford's stable, where three horses were together, and killed the centre horse, thirty-one shrapnel bullets being found in it. The others were untouched, as were also the men all round.

10th. Game Tree fort has begun with high velocity twelve-pounders. These are pernicious guns. Old Creaky can be provided for. She is carefully watched from everywhere — if she is pointed a bell rings, when the smoke comes from her muzzle another bell rings, and everybody goes to ground till the shell does (or does not) burst. But these smokeless guns give no warning; the report and the shell arrive simultaneously. Twenty-seven

shells were fired in a very short time round
the fort, three burst in it, and one knocked
a bucket from a nigger. But when they had
got the range accurately the Boers desisted.
Their artillery tactics are marvellous. They
fire in a casual way at anything; if they get the
range accurately they seem satisfied, and begin
to shoot at something else. They keep on
shooting for some time and unexpectedly
stop; then just as vaguely begin again, with
apparently no ulterior object, but general
annoyance. One thing only is certain, that
from 4.30 to 5 a.m. Creaky will fire a round
or two, and probably stop till after breakfast,
and that from 8.30 to 9 p.m. she has never
missed her farewell shot.

11th.   Shelling all day, sniping getting
really lively.

12th.   News of Colonel Plumer's column.
We were all grieved to hear of poor Black-
burne's death.

13th.   Slight shell fire, very quiet all round.

14th.   Sniping and shelling rather lively,
to compensate for yesterday.

15th.   Very quiet. Heavy rain during the
night ; the Boers entrenching themselves

4

towards the brickfields. An American despatch rider of Reuter's, Mr. Pearson, arrived, having ridden from south of Kimberley—a great performance.

16th. Heavy thunderstorm and rain; shelling and sniping all round.

17th. Shelling and sniping. The big gun again shifted rather farther back. Mr. Pearson started on his adventurous ride back to Cape Town. I wish him every success.

18th. To-day is the beginning of the end, I hope. Cronje's laager to the south-west is breaking up and trekking south. All squadrons have been warned to be in readiness to start at once, and we hope our turn is coming at last, but General Cronje is capable of any ruse to draw us out and endeavour to overwhelm us in the open. They do not forget to leave us Creaky, who gave us a heavy doing to-day; sniping is going on continually daily on our south-eastern and eastern front.

At this point of the siege it is worth while to review the situation. The Boers have been compelled to detach a large portion of their force to the south, leaving, however, ample men to invest the town. They have had four severe lessons and seem more disinclined than ever to come to close quarters. They have, however, entrenched themselves in suitable positions round the town, and it is impossible to say at any given point what their strength might be. Our strength is about nine hundred rifles, including all available white men, and a sortie, even if successful, might seriously impair our strength; whereas, as we are, we can hold the town, which is our primary object. For a sortie at the most we could only hope for two hundred to two hundred and fifty men, and the rapidity with which the Boers concentrate, and their vast superiority in artillery, would give them a very good chance of inflicting a defeat, which might be ruinous. No! their shell and musketry fire is annoying, but with the precautions that have been taken they cannot inflict sufficient damage to compel surrender. Thus, the whole thing resolves itself into a matter of " patience, our turn is coming soon.'' For if we cannot get out, neither they nor three times their number can get in.

From this time on till the begininng of December it may be as well to explain the situa-

4 *

tion in advance. The fighting on the western
and southern fronts had almost ceased, but the
Boer entrenchments were occupied by picquets,
who indulged in occasional sniping, and it
was unknown how many were in the rear of
them. The fort to the north, Game Tree fort,
was armed with a five-pounder gun, and was
occupied fairly strongly, and between that
and the waterworks was another trench,
occupied by the Boers, from which they were
eventually ousted by the fire of the Bechuanaland Rifles. To our eastern front lay the
trench by the race-course, strongly held; and
south of that in front of McMullen's farm
(the Boer main laager), a trench about thirteen
hundred yards from the town. There are four
or five brick-kilns about eleven to twelve
hundred yards from the town, running in
a diagonal direction from the trench down
towards the Molopo, and it was about here
that the continuous skirmishing took place ;
our works being pushed out to meet theirs
from the bed of the river, which was connected
with the town by a trench running due
south from Ellis's corner, past the old
Dutch church. Their guns were admirably

placed for raking the town, stadt, and defences on the south-eastern heights, about three thousand yards from the town. To the south of the river the Cape boys occupied a trench, near the eastern end of location, and about two thousand yards from the enemy's big gun.

19th, Sunday. Band and calls. Laager, to the north-east at Signal Hill, trekking eastward.

20th to 23rd. Daily shelling and sniping. Captain Sandford moved the Boers and the seven-pounders from the western entrenchments. One of these guns they now abandoned with the exception of a picquet.

24th. Shelling and sniping ; the B. S. A. P. fort came in for most of it ; two men wounded.

26th, Sunday. We had our first game of polo, a concert, and a football match. Church in the evening.

27th. An advanced trench had been constructed in the river bed, six hundred yards from the Boer trench, and fourteen hundred yards from the big gun : Lord Charles Bentinck occupied it after dark.

28th. The big gun was harassed by volleys
all day, and did not fire much, a lively
skirmish going on at intervals throughout the
day on the eastern front, Maxims, guns and
rifles; Cape Boys partaking from the south of
the Molopo. Fitzclarence relieved Lord
Charles Bentinck this evening. The Boers
vacated the brick-kilns after the firing had
been going on for some time.

29th. The long-range volleys have undoubtedly had good effect. The big gun
cocked up her nose and fired two rounds
wildly this morning. On the eastern front was
a crowd with telescopes and field glasses,
laughing at the gunners, who could plainly
be seen dodging about, and making many futile
efforts to get off their piece safely somehow.
Ellis's corner, Fitzclarence's squadron, the Cape
Boys in the river bed and in the trench,
volleyed him directly old Creaky's muzzle was
elevated. The enemy could not find out
where the fire came from, and fired their
smaller guns and one-pound Maxim, on chance,
all about the place, but did no harm. Creaky
only got off three rounds to-day. When the
Boers in the trench tried to join in, the Maxim

at Ellis's corner was turned on to them;
while the Maxim from De Kock's fort paid a
similar attention to the race-course trenches.
The Boers in the north-west also shelled to-
day. Lord Charles Bentinck relieved Fitzclarence after dark.

30th. This was the hottest day's firing we
have had for some time. At 3 a.m. a heavy
fire commenced all round. The Boers had been
annoyed by our native snipers in the river
and brickfields, and commenced firing so-called
volleys from their trench in the direction of
the river bed. The Cape Boys and the
squadron fired on the big gun and Ellis's
corner fired on the Boers. Our Hotchkiss also
fired, but the seven-pounder gun, concealed in
the bed of the river, did not fire, but awaited
developments, as its position was still unknown
to the enemy ; this went on with short intervals all day, but an hour and an half before
sundown began a most furious fusillade all
round. Creaky, who had now been furnished
with cover for her gunners, joined in the fray,
and for over an hour heavy firing was
incessant, and a very pretty fight followed.
In all this firing on the south-eastern corner

the bullets drop in the town, and the market square and surrounding streets are no places for a contemplative stroll at these times. The other day, during a game of football, a ninety-four-pound shell passed through the players and burst in the town house, in the centre of the square, but marvellous to relate, none were injured though the interior of the town house has disappeared. To return to the skirmish, after a vast expenditure of ammunition our casualties were nil ; I trust the enemy's were heavy. In a Transvaal paper, dated December 2nd, they confessed to several being slightly wounded lately by our continuous fire.

December 1st. To check an undesirable expenditure of ammunition, Colonel Baden-Powell detailed an officer, Mr. Greenfield and six men to accompany the Cape Boys (who invariably opened the ball) up the river bed with orders not to fire unless sure of killing some one, because, though they thoroughly enjoyed themselves yesterday they got through an enormous quantity of powder and shot. These Cape Boys are good men, fair shots, very brave, and have accounted for quite a large number of Boers while out sniping. In consequence of these orders sniping resumed its old condition, and not many volleys were fired. Creaky, in consequence, fired rather more.

2nd. The fire of the Bechuanaland Rifles drove the Boers from their advanced trench to the north-east, which they had occupied, but subsequently abandoned and destroyed, as it was too advanced. But another trench was constructed midway between this trench and our own advanced trench. Four railway men out sniping towards Game Tree fort, came upon the niggers the Boers had posted in advance of that earthwork, and shot one, the rest fled. The Boers swarmed into the trench and their commander was heard to order some men to go and cut the party off. Sharp came the answer, " No, the rooineks are attacking in force." Eventually, after crawling a thousand yards under fire, the party got off safely, having accounted for two Boers.

3rd, Sunday. As our parties were digging late Saturday night and early this morning in the vicinity of the Boer trenches the Boers sent in a flag this morning to ask if we meant

to fight on Sunday. We sent back to say no.
I rode round the western outpost from the outside and was much struck by the admirable
way Major Godley had laid out the trenches; they
were practically impregnable. I also went up
to Cannon Kopje which, with infinite difficulty,
has been much strengthened daily, or, I should
say, nightly. We then had sports, tilting at the
ring, tent-pegging, &c., two pony races, and
a polo match, and all the rank and fashion of
Mafeking assembled to partake of Colonel
Hore's and the Protectorate Regiment's hos-
pitality, and to "listen to the band." The
only thing that has been thoroughly levelled
in Mafeking is the Polo ground, which is very
fair, and the ponies surprisingly good. Practising polo, and mounted sports, however,
have been forbidden during week days, as it
draws so much fire. Indeed, Creaky elevated
her muzzle once during the afternoon, which
caused a certain amount of sensation, as we do
not exactly trust our foes, and one shell in the
crowd would have secured a good bag. It
was probably to show her to the Dutch ladies
who drive out to their camp on Sunday. These
ladies have ceased watching the effects of the

shells on the town since long range volleys began. Church in the evening. Sunday is indeed a welcome fillip all round, particularly for the poor women and children, who are confined to the laager all the week ; eleven of the latter have died since the commencement of the siege. There are services for all denominations, every Sunday ; but I think the evening ones are the more plentifully attended.

4th. A quiet day ; not much shelling or sniping.

5th. Shelling and sniping. A shell burst in Well's store, killing a nigger outside (at least he died afterwards), close to me. The pieces flew all about, and I had not time to analyse where they were falling ; they came too quick, but it was a pretty close shave ; but then there have been innumerable close shaves and marvellous little damage done to life so far. The shell passed through the roof, just below the look-out man, whom the shot threw into the air. Fortunately it exploded in the next store, otherwise no doubt he would have been blown to pieces. As I write two shells have just exploded, one blowing a Kaffir to pieces and wrecking a chemist shop, the other knocking over a white man, who is just being removed to hospital; how much hurt I do not know. (I hear that he was killed.) About 3 o'clock began the most tremendous rain, which lasted for two hours, the market square became a lake, the streets rivers, whilst our little Molopo developed at short notice into a raging torrent. It swept away all impedimenta, wooden bridges, &c., at once. The squadron in the river bed had to retire and Captain Fitzclarence while endeavouring to cross was nearly drowned. The seven-pounder was nearly washed away; the ammunition was. The trenches and bomb proofs were full to the brim, many of them proving to be in the beds of regular streams. Had the Boers known or been able to seize their opportunity they might have made it very nasty for us with shell fire, but as it was they were in a worse plight than we were, as they had no dry cover for drying their clothes, and could not replace them, and when they emerged from their trenches our Maxims opened on them. The headquarters' staff set to work and had everybody fairly comfortable by 7 o'clock. Natives were at work bailing all night; dry clothes were given to those who had no change, brandy and quinine served out to all the trenches, the men sleeping in adjacent cover. Wagons fetched up the women from the laager, and blankets were distributed to all who required them. As usual all rose to the occasion, and having proved themselves under fire now repeated the process under this onslaught from water. Perhaps the people who were worst off were the B. S. A. P. at Cannon Kopje. A wet night—their shelters flooded—and literally everything they possessed carried away, except their blankets, arms and the clothes they stood up in, and no shelter at all. However, take it all round, the enemy were much worse off than we, which is always consoling, and consequently being miserable, and having nothing to do, they opened a lively fire on the town generally, lasting about half an hour.

6th. Shelling and sniping as usual. It is their custom now to begin in the evening about 4, keep it up till dark, and then fire Creaky once from about 8.30 to 9 o'clock. Mr. Gerrans, town councillor, was extracting the fuse of an exploded shell—result—he was blown down and severely injured. His foreman, Green, had his foot blown off, and

a passer by, Smith, a Johannesburg refugee,
returning to his trench, was so injured that he
died in an hour. Everybody was much
depressed by this; it seemed so sad that more
damage should be caused among the whites
by an accident than had hitherto been the
result of six weeks' shelling by the enemy's
heavy gun. However, since artillery has been
invented mankind will tamper with loaded
shells, in spite of all warnings, orders, or
entreaties to the contrary.

7th. Lady Sarah Wilson arrived this
morning, having been exchanged for Viljoen
who had been sentenced to six months'
imprisonment before the war began. He,
I fancy, will look fatter and in better condition
than his friends outside, and did not appear
over keen to join them. This plucky lady
was received with loud cheers when she
entered the town; she has indeed had a bad
time, and everybody was greatly relieved to
see her back safely, though perhaps this is not
quite the best place that I know of to have
a villa residence. As she drove up to her
house the firing commenced again—they did
not waste much time. Heavy shelling con-

tinued after dark. Three men killed, eight wounded.

Apropos of shells, I presume in the course of his life Colonel Baden-Powell has had many curious communications, but certainly none more curious than this one. The other morning a Kaffir picked up an unexploded five-pound shell; when the fuse was unscrewed, instead of a charge the following missive was found :—

" Mr. Baden-Powell,

Pleas excuse me for sending this iron messenger i have no other to send at Present. He is rather exentric but vorgive him if he does not behave well i wish to ask you not to let your men drink all the whisky as i wish to have a drink when we all come to see you. cindly tell Mrs. Dunkley that her mother and vamily are all quite well.

I remaijn, Yours trewly, a Republican."

I am afraid the ingenious gentleman in question will have to wait a while for his whisky.

8th. Quiet all the morning; but this afternoon shell fire began, killing one man, Protectorate Regiment, and wounding two.

Creaky only fired one round, our snipers keeping her quiet; but sniping all round made things pretty lively.

9th. Pretty quiet ; not much shell fire in the morning, but began in the evening, and pretty smart sniping continued all day. I must now endeavour to describe the hospital arrangements, and the noble work done by the ladies of Mafeking. The hospital arrangements for the defence of the town were made under the supervision of Dr. Haves, Major Anderson, R.A.M.C., and Surgeon Holmden assisting him; Major Anderson being attached to the Protectorate Regiment, which might have been moved at any time. In addition to being under a hot fire the whole of the first fight, he accompanied the ambulance to Cannon Kopje, during the fight there. Bullets whistled round the Red Cross the whole way there and round the stretchers (which he assisted to carry) on their return to the shelter of the railway embankment. There may have been some excuse for firing on the Red Cross during the first fight, on the second occasion there can have been none ; probably the Boers considered that we adopted the same practice as themselves and brought up our ammunition in ambulances. Whether this is a valid excuse or not, I will leave my readers to decide. The Red Cross flag, at the commencement of the siege floated over the railway embankment, the first dressing station, the refugee camp dressing station, the women's laager, Messrs. Weil's (who had placed their house at the disposal of the authorities for the use of the wounded), the convent, which is fitted up as a hospital, and the Victoria Hospital. General Cronje stated, and with some show of reason, that he could only recognize one hospital, and the women's laager. However, prior to this, he had sent many shells through the convent, possibly from its being a two-storied building and naturally a conspicuous mark. Consequently Victoria Hospital, always the main hospital, became the only one used throughout the operations. Dr. Haves was the P. M. O., Miss Hill the matron; and here, on behalf of the garrison of Mafeking, I must endeavour to convey our feelings of deep gratitude and admiration for the work done by this lady, the nurses, and their assistants

5

(the ladies of Mafeking) during the siege. I can testify personally to their devoted care and attention to patients, and Britain may well be proud of them. One ninety-four pounder went through the hospital, wrecking a ward and killing a little native boy. Shells fell all round it, and bullets were continually hitting it, one, indeed, wounded an already wounded man, but these ladies continued their work undisturbed, assisted to the utmost by the sisters from the adjacent convent, situated some fifty yards away. These poor ladies having had to abandon their home (which was literally wrecked, and will have to be entirely rebuilt), had to take refuge in a dug-out by the hospital. The hospital arrangements and the attention of Dr. Haves, Major Anderson, and Surgeon Holmden (who was himself sick in the hospital), were beyond all praise. Fortunately the accommodation was adequate, an additional building being erected for Kaffirs. But these for the most part preferred being treated and returning to their own abode. They appear nearly insensible to pain.

To give a few instances, one native was shot

with a Martini bullet through the lung; he roared with laughter when it was extracted, and will not part with it for anything, and is now all right. A Zulu wounded in the toe, on seeing a man's temperature being taken, when given the thermometer, placed it between his toes, and on being told to put it in his mouth, said he was not hurt in the mouth, but in the foot. Another native was shot through the head with a Mauser and lived ; so, indeed, did a railway volunteer, Nelson ; the bullet went clean through his head, and he is well and out of hospital. But the natives, though suffering from horrible injuries, seem to regard them lightly. Most of the native wounded are by shells ; they are very careless, but I fancy the numerous casualties are making them more cautious. The unfortunate man killed yesterday was a man named Footman, of the Protectorate Regiment, who was in a room singing a song, " Poor old Joe has gone to rest," to the accompaniment of a banjo, when the shell burst on him, and literally blew him to pieces—two more men were slightly injured, and a chaff-cutter knocked to pieces ; but the remainder were providentially untouched.

The worst of sniping is that it consumes such a
lot of the ammunition which we may eventually
require, though it certainly has a quietening
effect upon the enemy's artillery ; but I cannot
believe the Boers will abandon this place
without one more serious attack, when they
hear of the advance of our troops, and the
remnants of other commandoes join them.
They must have one tangible proof of success.
So far, beyond doubt, the prolonged defence
of Mafeking has resulted in the natives either
keeping quiet or rising on our side, whereas
had the Boers been successful in these parts,
the natives must have perforce sided with
them, as their emissaries had strained every
nerve to induce them to do, prior to the war.
I sincerely trust that the penalties of treason
will be rigidly enforced, and that if not death,
at least outlawry and confiscation will be
inflicted on the Colonial Dutch who have
risen, for no man has a right to a vote who
has deliberately risen in British territory and
fought against Her Majesty. The Transvaal is another matter, though they have
raided our territory, burnt farms, and looted
cattle and annexed British Bechuanaland—

that is a matter for settlement by the Government and not for individuals to suffer. If the Boers are well thrashed, and they have fought well, the two nationalities will soon settle down together. But a Dutchman, or at least the lower classes (which correspond, after all, to poor whites of America with this difference, that they have a lot of black blood in them), cannot understand anything but a good licking. Disarm them rigorously, and give them a just government and they will soon peacefully acquiesce therein. But pack the Hollander-cum-German official back to his own country. South Africa is no place for them. Let them try the South American Republics; with their venal habits, they will be thoroughly at home.

A more heterogeneous garrison has seldom been collected. A mounted corps (the Protectorate Regiment), two detachments of mounted Cape Police, the B. S. A. P., also mounted, the Bechuanaland Rifles, the Railway D. W., and the Town Guard, all employed in trenches, and the horses only used for orderly work. The Town Guard is composed of every white man or householder,

Indian or otherwise, capable of bearing arms, unless enrolled under the Red Cross. They are formed into companies in their own districts, and under their own commanders, Colonel Vyvyan being commander of the whole, and range from boys of sixteen to men of seventy. The younger boys are employed as messengers. The Town Guard have been subjected to severe tests, sleeping and living in trenches, and enduring the hardships of war for two months, without a chance of returning the enemy's fire. A few individuals who are good shots are permitted to go out sniping, but the majority have to keep their fire for short ranges, in case of an assault. They have done their duty well, and been under fire continually. All sorts and conditions of men are there, and a more mixed body it would be impossible to conceive. In any case, they have stood the test well, and surprised myself and indeed everybody by their efficiency. Of the police of both corps, it is impossible to say too much—they are as fine a body of men as you could wish to see, and the work they have done speaks for itself. The B. S. A. P.

have had the more opportunities as a body,
but wherever the Cape Police have had
a chance they have done every bit as well.
The Protectorate Regiment I have already
described fully, and they also have proved
themselves to be the fine fighting material
I thought them from the first. But when,
oh! when, shall we use our horses ? The
Bechuanaland Rifles, a fine body of men,
largely augmented since the commencement
of the war, had a mounted detachment under
Captain Cowell. The Railway Division
under Captain Moore, who has been promoted
since the commencement of the war, are also
a fine body of men who can turn their hand
to anything, from fighting in a land ironclad
to manning their own works. The authorities were warned long prior to the outbreak of hostilities, that more troops were
required here. With even two squadrons of
cavalry and half a battery we should have
been able to keep the Boers at a greater
distance from the town, and beaten them
occasionally in the open, well away from our
lines. Half a battalion of infantry would
have done the garrison work as efficiently

as the dismounted men of our mounted corps. In fact, we might long ago have raised the siege by a decisive blow, which we have been, under our present circumstances, unable to deliver. I think I stated this in a letter some six weeks prior to the outbreak of the war. However, I presume we shall soon be out of this now, though we have no news, as for the past fortnight no runners seem able to get through at all.

10th, Sunday. We had mounted sports, polo, and in the evening, church. Heavy rain threatened, but held off. I watched through a telescope a party of Dutch ladies being shown Creaky, who was put through her antics, being elevated, depressed, levelled in various directions, for their benefit. So, both sides enjoyed themselves after their kind.

General Snyman's harangues and reports of victories (which roughly surmised are—extirpation of the British army—the only two places in South Africa held by the British, being Mafeking and Cape Town—possession of Delagoa Bay, and a fight at sea, where the British were defeated) are now received in silence and *cum grano*, by his followers, instead of being greeted with cheers, as formerly. Really, I begin to believe there *is* a limit to the credulity of the Boer, though hitherto I had supposed it boundless. But what can equal their colossal impudence, in invading the suzerain power, annexing Bechuanaland, and proclaiming us rebels. Colonel Baden-Powell has recently organized a troop of old cavalry soldiers, and armed them with lances. They have to-day ridden all round the town, showing themselves in all quarters, to the great astonishment of the Boers, who, I suppose, now expect another little surprise packet, and will be anxious for a few days; as they knew we had no lances with us.

11th, Monday. Colonel Baden-Powell has issued a proclamation calling upon all burghers to return to their farms by the 14th, and that if they do so, and surrendered their rifles and one hundred and fifty rounds of ammunition, they will not be molested, otherwise, they will be treated most rigorously, when we take the offensive; that they are being grossly misled by their leaders; that foreign intervention is hopeless. The Staats Artillery may surrender as prisoners of war at any time; this does not apply to British subjects, traitors or deserters. This might have produced an increase of shell fire, I should fancy, judging from our heavy days' shelling last week. Their General rode forth with his escort, our snipers placed three volleys round him, whereupon he galloped back to the big gun, and all the artillery began merrily, trying to hit our headquarters. They fired a few shells this morning, but the heavy rain seriously damped their ardour. Still, if the General be annoyed, they will probably re-commence their attentions. Later. The orderlies with the various flags of truce, have returned, proclamations were sent to each of their out-works, and all the Dutchmen volunteered that they were quite sick of it, and had had enough, which I can quite believe. The rains are beginning, they complained of the soakings they have already had, and with inadequate cover sickness will soon play havoc with them. The orderlies gave them cigarettes and conversed with them, and in two or three cases they asked them how they came to let the re-inforcements in, referring to the lancer troop. In one case the Dutchman said he had heard them come in, but did not know what it was, in the other cases they said they had not seen the re-inforcements, but they had seen their spoor. Shelling has recommenced. To-night we send up fire balloons, weather permitting, which will probably produce some effect on their side.

The following is a copy of Colonel Baden-Powell's letter to Snyman and the proclamation to the burghers :—

A LETTER TO THE BOERS.

Mafeking, 8th Dec., 1899.

To General J. P. Snyman,

near Mafeking.

SIR,—I beg to thank you for having handed over Lady Sarah Wilson in exchange for the convict P. Viljoen.

At the same time, I beg to point out that I have only consented to the exchange under protest, as being contrary to the custom of civilised warfare.

In treating this lady as a prisoner of war, as well as in various other acts, you have in the present campaign, altered the usual conditions of war. This is a very serious matter ; and I do not know whether it has the sanction of General Joubert or not, but I warn you of the consequences.

The war was at first, and would remain, as far as Her

Majesty's troops are concerned, a war between one Government and another; but you are making it one of people against people in which women are considered as belligerents. I warn you that the consequence of this may shortly be very serious to your own people, and you yourself will be to blame for anything that may happen.

Regarding your complaint as to your being attacked by Natives, I beg to refer you to my letter dated 14th November, addressed to your predecessor General Cronje. In this letter I went out of my way, as one white man to another, to warn you that the Natives are becoming extremely incensed at your stealing their cattle, and the wanton burning of their Kraals; they argued that the war lay only between our two Nations, and that the quarrel had nothing to do with themselves, and they had remained neutral in consequence, excepting in the case of the Mafeking Baralongs, who had to defend their homes in consequence of your unjustifiable invasion. Nevertheless you thought fit to carry on cattle thefts and raids against them, and you are now beginning to feel the consequences; and, as I told you, I could not be responsible. And I fear from what I have just heard by wireless telegraph that the Natives are contemplating further operations should your Forces continue to remain within or on the borders of their territories. Before the commencement of the war the High Commissioner issued stringent orders to all Natives that they were to remain quiet and not to take up Arms unless their territory were invaded (in which case, of course, they had a perfect right to defend themselves).

Linchwe—of whom you complain—remained neutral until you brought a force into his principal town and looted his traders' stores, and were making preparations for shelling his stadt on the 26th ultimo. Having obtained accurate information of these intentions of yours, and warned by what had happened to the Natives near Mafeking, he attacked your laager on the 24th in order to save his town from being shelled and consequent loss of life amongst his women and children. In this I consider he was quite justified, and you have no one but yourself to blame in the matter.

While on the subject of Natives please do not suppose that I am ignorant of what you have been doing with regard to seeking the assistance of armed natives, nor of the use of the Natives by you in the destruction of the railway line south of Mafeking. However, having done my duty in briefly giving you warning on these points, I do not propose to further discuss them by letter.

I have the honour to be,

Sir,

Your obedient servant,

R. S. S. BADEN-POWELL.

NOTICE

TO THE BURGHERS OF THE Z. A. R. AT PRESENT UNDER ARMS NEAR MAFEKING.

From the Officer Commanding Her Majesty's Forces, Mafeking.

BURGHERS,—I address you in this manner because

I have only recently learnt how you are being intentionally kept in the dark by your officers and your Government newspapers as to what is really happening in other parts of South Africa.

As officer commanding Her Majesty's troops on this border I think it right to point out to you clearly the inevitable result of your remaining any longer in arms against Great Britain.

You are all aware that the present war was caused by the invasion of British territory by your forces, and as most of you know, without any justifiable reason.

Your leaders do not tell you that so far your forces have met with what is only the advanced guard of the British force, and that circumstances have changed within the past week; the main body of the British is now daily arriving by thousands from England, Canada, India, and Australia, and is about to advance through your country. In a few weeks the South African Republic will be in the hands of the English; no sacrifice of life on your part can stop it. The question now to put to yourselves before it is, is this : Is it worth while losing your lives in a vain attempt to stop their invasion or to take a town beyond your borders which, if taken, would be of no use to you ? (And I may tell you that Mafeking cannot be taken by sitting down and looking at it, for we have ample supplies for several months to come).

The Staat Artillery have done us very little damage, and we are now well protected with forts and mines. Your presence here, or elsewhere, under arms, cannot stop the British advancing into your country.

Your leaders and newspapers are also trying to make you believe that some foreign continental powers are likely to intervene in your behalf against England. This is not in keeping with their pretence that your side is going to be victorious, nor is it in accordance with facts. The S. A. R. having declared war and taken the offensive cannot claim intervention on its behalf. And were it not so, the German Emperor is at present in England, and fully in sympathy with us : the American Government have warned others of their intention to side with England should any other nation interfere ; France has large interests in the gold fields identical with those of England ; and Italy is entirely in accord with us; and Russia sees no cause to interfere.

The war is a war of one Government against another and not of people against people. The duty assigned to my troops is to sit still here until the proper time arrives and then to fight and to kill until you give in. You, on the other hand, have other interests to think of, in your families and farms and their safety.

Your leaders have caused the destruction of farms in this country and have fired on women and children, and our men are becoming hard to restrain in consequence. Your leaders have also caused invasion of Kaffir territory, and looting of their cattle, and have thus induced them to rise, and in their turn to invade your country, and to kill your burghers. As one white man to another, I warned General Cronje on the 14th November that this would occur, and yesterday I heard that more Kaffirs are rising, and are contemplating similar moves; and I have warned Snyman accordingly. Thus great bloodshed, and destruction of farms threaten you on all sides, and I wish to offer you a chance of avoiding it. To this end my advice to you is to return without delay to your homes and there remain peacefully till the war is over. Those of you who do this before the 14th instant will be as far as possible protected, as regards yourselves, your families, and property, from confiscations, looting, and other penalties to which those who remain under arms may be subjected when the invasion takes place.

Our secret agents will communicate to me the names of those who do and of those who do not avail themselves, before the 13th instant, of the terms now offered.

To ensure their property being respected, all the men of a family must be present at home when the troops arrive and be prepared to hand over a rifle and 150 rounds of ammunition each.

The above terms do not apply to officers or to members of the Staats Artillery, who may surrender as prisoners of war at any time; nor do they apply to rebels from British territory or others against whom there may be other charges. It is probable that my force will shortly again take the offensive.

To those who, after this warning, defer their submission till too late, I can offer no promise, and they will only have themselves to blame for an injury or loss of property that they or their families may afterwards suffer.

(Signed)   R. S. S. BADEN-POWELL,
Colonel.

MAFEKING, 10*th Dec.*, 1899.

The proclamation has either had a good effect or it is a curious coincidence, that, since its issue, the town has been barely shelled at all, sniping has almost ceased, and the Boers have only shelled the trenches in front of the native location, and the location itself, in a perfunctory manner, the result being that though we have shot a few Boers, our casualties have been nil, except some natives in the location, and from the 12th to the 15th nothing worth mentioning has happened. I fancy their news from the south must be bad, and undoubtedly men and cattle have gone away lately. Thanks to their recent vigilance, our native runners have failed to get through, and I imagine the same fate has befallen the runners trying to come in, for we have been absolutely without reliable news for the last three weeks. General Snyman sent in a copy of the *Volkstem*, relating our enormities and their victories, all underlined. I am bound to say the news was taken with much salt; but still it was news of a sort. The leading articles were mainly whining for foreign intervention, so we could read between the lines.

6

15th. Later. I was somewhat previous in my remarks, they have just placed a shell within a hundred yards of the hotel.

December 16th. (Dingaan Day.) We were aroused at 2.39 a.m. by the Boers celebrating their independence. They sent a ninety-four pounder through the corner of Dixon's Hotel, which is our headquarters, consequently all rooms and passages are full of sleepers, the orderlies sleeping in the passages and billiard room. However, fortunately they managed to put their shell through the bar, which is the only empty room in the house, and wrecked a portion of it and the stoep, which by day is full of occupants. A splinter stopped the town clock, hence the accuracy with which we timed our unlooked-for alarum. They have tried to hit headquarters for some weeks, shells pitching all round the hotel and wrecking neighbouring buildings, but heretofore we had escaped. Then, having drawn their bow at a venture by night, they have at last succeeded in hitting it. After having inspected the damage I turned in again. But as our seven-pounder at Cannon Kopje returned the fire, it became universal, and I think the Boers intended to attack. Colonel Baden-Powell having anticipated something of the sort, had had the little gun laid on their big one the night before. As it was impossible to sleep, I went down to Ellis's corner to join in the fun. For nearly three weeks we had let them fire away without taking much notice of them. To-day, however, knowing it was their national festival, we were determined to disturb their amusement. Our old seven-pounders had their advanced trenches well in range, and three of them, about three-quarters of a mile apart, commenced playing havoc with the said trenches, shells bursting beautifully in and over them. While Creaky, like a big dog annoyed by little ones, snapped hurriedly at each of its puny antagonists in turn. It made better practice than I have yet seen, and burst its huge shells within fifteen and twenty yards of the guns. When the smoke from its muzzle was seen, our gun detachments laid down, but the explosion and smoke of the big shells had not died away before "boom," through the smoke, came the derisive return of its tiny antagonist, showing "a miss to the Boers."

6 *

The guns took no notice of Creaky after the first shot, but concentrated their attention on the trenches, leaving her to be soothed by musketry volleys. Our shell fire had a most quieting effect on the occupants of the trenches, and we had to stir them up by sniping their individuals, and then when they woke up a bit the Maxims assisted in calming their unruly spirits again. Altogether a most enjoyable morning. It is so dull being shot at without answering, but when one's own guns keep the game going, it is quite another thing. This lasted till about 6.30. Just to prevent their being too much taken up by any amusements they might have contemplated, to celebrate the day, our guns fired a few rounds again at noon, but the big gun only answered with a few rounds, and after a feeble spatter of musketry we knocked off. On the western front, about dusk, our seven-pounder, under Captain Sandford, knocked out their five-pounder, and they dismantled their fort and withdrew to a more retired position.

We have advanced our seven-pounder to Fort Ayr, and hope to repeat the process.

REMOVING THE EFFECTS OF A BOER SHELL.

By permission of "The Daily Graphic."

The first of our shells burst right among them whilst they were outside making coffee.

17th, Sunday. We had a handicap polo tournament. Here are the teams and the result from *The Mafeking Mail* :—

No. I.—Colonel Baden-Powell (Captain),
    Captain Gordon Wilson,
    Captain Singleton,
    Lieutenant Hon. A. Hanbury-Tracey.

No. II.—Captain Lord C. Cavendish - Bentinck
    (Captain),
    Lieutenant-Colonel Walford,
    Major Anderson,
    Lieutenant Mackenzie.

No. III.—Lieutenant-Colonel Hore (Captain),
    Captain Sandford,
    Captain Vernon,
    Lieutenant Bridges.

No. IV.—Major Godley (Captain),
    Major Goold-Adams, C.B., C.M.G.,
    Captain Fitzclarence,
    Lieutenant Moncreiffe.

No. V.—Major Baillie (Captain),
    Captain Marsh,
    Captain Cowan,
    Lieutenant Paton.

Match.		Goals scored.
1	Colonel Hore . . .	1
	Lord C. Bentinck . .	1
2	Colonel Baden-Powell .	0
	Major Godley . . .	1
3	Lord C. Bentinck . .	1
	Major Baillie . . .	1
4	Colonel Baden-Powell .	0
	Colonel Hore . . .	1
5	Major Godley . . .	0
	Major Baillie . . .	2
6	Lord C. Bentinck . .	0
	Colonel Baden-Powell .	1
7	Major Godley . . .	1
	Colonel Hore . . .	1
8	Major Baillie . . .	0
	Colonel Baden-Powell .	1
9	Lord C. Bentinck . .	1
	Major Godley . . .	0
10	Major Baillie . . .	1
	Colonel Hore . . .	0

	Total goals scored.
Colonel Baden-Powell's team . .	2
Captain Lord C. Bentinck's team . .	3
Lieutenant-Colonel Hore's team . .	3
Major Baillie's team	4
Major Godley's team	2

Colonel Baden-Powell's team had a Captain who played an excellent game. Major Baillie was decidedly the mainstay of his team, not only by the unerring accuracy with which he hit the ball, but also on account of the verbal assistance delivered unceasingly in stentorian tones to his side.

We are now making great preparations for Christmas, which we are apparently condemned to spend here. Church services as usual.

18th. A quiet day; except on the western front, where their five-pounder keeps pegging away; however, no one takes any notice of it, as our new gun-pit is not yet completed. To-morrow we hope to have another lively morning. The Boers have been drilling, apparently practising an attack formation, somewhat late in the day, however, and not of much use now, as they could not get in if they tried, and they are not likely to make the attempt. As I before said, Colonel Baden-Powell has collected some thirty lances and armed a troop with them, so that, if the enemy depart hurriedly, we may be able to speed them on their way. Went sniping in the evening; they fired the one-pound Maxim and a good deal of musketry fire. Our troops in the advance trenches had quite good shooting all day.

19th. As I anticipated. The Boers' *reveille*

was sounded for them at 4.30 a.m. by our seven-pounders, which made excellent practice on the brickfield trench. Their big gun repeated its performance of Saturday harmlessly. We shifted them from their trenches and turned Maxims on them, while the Nordenfeldt at long range volleys pestered their big gun. Their one-pound Maxim fire was wild, but they slew an inoffensive jackass. This lasted until about 6, and was very pretty. At about 7 Creaky began to fire at Cannon Kopje, but without effect; she shot straighter in the morning; and at about 9 our seven-pounders began again, but the enemy would not be drawn, and now only occasional dropping shots come idly from both sides. On the western front our seven-pounder silenced the five-pounder at Game Tree fort. On the eastern front the race-course trench much annoyed the gun under Major Panzera, with volleys, till kept under by the convent Maxim and our one-pound Maxim. These two artillery fights cannot much impress the Boers with the extraordinary value of the much belauded ten-tonner, and must destroy her moral effect, for whichever of our guns she fires at immediately returns her fire. However, she has annoyed us quite enough and done sufficient damage to life and property, but if we had only had a gun which could have reached her properly, we should have knocked her out long ago. A duel between our Nordenfeldt and Creaky began this afternoon, and has since been of daily occurrence, amidst the laughter and applause of the spectators. No sooner has the big shell struck, than crack, crack, comes from the Nordenfeldt. Indeed, of late the little gun fires when the smoke from Creaky's muzzle appears, and gets off its three shots before the arrival of the shell, which the gunners of the monster do not seem to appreciate at all. It is a regular case of dignity and impudence with the laugh on the side of impudence. In the evening Captain Sandford silenced the Boer gun on the western front.

20th and 21st. Quiet days.

22nd. Quiet, but furious musketry fire at night, bullets flying everywhere.

23rd, Saturday. Fairly quiet.

I broke my head taking a fall at polo, which we now play two or three times a week ; it is a new experience going to and from the polo ground under fire.

24th, Sunday. Owing to siege exigencies it was deemed necessary to hold our Christmas on the Sunday, as the Boers' religious festival is held on New Year's Day. All creeds held their ordinary Church services. Lady Sarah Wilson and Mr. B. Weil had organized a Christmas tree and tea for the two hundred and fifty children of Dutch and English parentage who were in the town. Brakes were running to and from the laager, filled with children, shrilly cheering and waving the Union Jack, the most effective one run by poor Captain Vernon, who was killed within forty-eight hours. The children seemed thoroughly to enjoy themselves, and great thanks are due to the organizers of the fête and their assistants, for everyone was pleased to see the children enjoy themselves. For the adults, sports were held, and a cheerful Christmas Day was passed.

Christmas Day. All creeds held their usual Christmas services though under some difficulty, as everyone was on duty, though the Boers kept Christmas as Sunday ; yet it was

no certainty to commence with. The Rev.
Mr. Weekes, the Church of England clergy-
man, had to play the harmonium as well as
conduct the service.

26th. The myriads of locusts which had
lately devastated our grazing grounds, already
insufficient for the large number of cattle in
and about the town, had rendered it imperative
that some steps should be taken to raise our
close investment sufficiently to obtain an
extended field for grazing secure from attack
or raid. This was sufficient reason for action
in itself, but in addition, the approach of our
forces to Gaberones in the north, made it
advisable to prepare to open up the line and
endeavour to join hands with them, and thus
by extending our perimeter and line of forts
to throw additional work on the investing
force, and so prevent reinforcements being
sent to the commandoes acting against our
troops north and south ; nay, we even hoped
to draw reinforcement from these commandoes
to assist in maintaining the strict investment
which the Boers deemed it so necessary
to retain around Mafeking. Accordingly,
Colonel Baden-Powell decided to attack Game

Tree fort, which commands the line to the
north. And now, before going further with
an account of the fight, let me say that in
spite of great secrecy, as to the time or place
of attack, the Boers, through treachery, were
forewarned and forearmed as to our intentions.
The garrison was doubled, and the fort from
an open earthwork turned into a block-house
with three tiers of fire, while the line was
broken in the night between the fort and the
town, preventing the efficient co-operation of
the armoured train. On Christmas night, at
about 11 o'clock, the chief of the staff, Lord
Edward Cecil, collected the correspondents
and told them of the intended attack, advising
them to rendezvous at 3 o'clock, with the
headquarters at Dummie fort. The plan of
attack was as follows :—C squadron, Protectorate Regiment, were to take up a position
during the night near the railway to the west
of Game Tree fort, supported by D squadron,
under Captain Fitzclarence, and the armoured
train with a Hotchkiss and Maxim, under
Captain Williams, B. S. A. P. The right
flank being protected by the Bechuanaland Rifles, under Captain Cowan. The

whole of the right attack under Major Godley. The left attack being composed of three seven-pounder guns, one cavalry Maxim, and one troop, Lord Charles Bentinck's A squadron, Protectorate Regiment, under Major Panzera, with the other two troops in support, the whole left attack being under Colonel Hore. The Dummie fort lay midway between the two attacks. The wait from 3 o'clock seemed interminable, but at 4.28 the first gun fired, and then our seven-pounder shells burst merrily over the fort. The infantry commenced volleys and the Maxim joined in. The armoured train was stopped by the broken line some half mile from where it could have efficiently co-operated, and the squadrons commenced their attack from the railway line, D being escheloned some three hundred yards in the rear of C. From the Dummie fort the attack could be perfectly seen, as it advanced rapidly across our front. The rushes were well made, and the charge in perfect order, the leaders racing in front of their men right up to the fort, where the firing for a while ceased, and then broke out again with renewed vigour.

From where I was, I thought the attacking
squadron had secured the position, and, from
the slowness and deliberation with which the
men retired, that the supporting squadron was
falling back to its lines, as, with the smokeless
powder, we could not see our men firing, and
the sound was drowned in the rattle of Boer
musketry. This, alas, was not the case.
Captain Vernon, who had been wounded in
the advance, led his men most gallantly up to
the work, to find it with three tiers of loop-
holes and an iron roof, the bushes in front
concealing this until right on to the fort. Here
he and Lieutenant Paton and fifteen men fell,
and his sergeant-major mortally wounded.
Captain Sandford had been shot twice just
short of the work, but called on his men to
charge. These were the last words he spoke,
and only four of the men of his troop were
not placed *hors de combat*. Captain Fitzclarence had also fallen wounded, before
reaching the work, but I am glad to say is
doing well. With this spirit shown by the
officers and responded to by the men,
small wonder that we may be proud
of the attack, even though unsuccessful in

obtaining possession of the work, and that
the Boers afterwards seemed more depressed
than ourselves. They knew the men they
had to deal with. Corporal Cooke got on the
roof of the work, and had four bullets through
his tunic, but was untouched. Mr. Paton and
Sergeant-Major Paget were shot whilst firing
with their revolvers through the loop-holes
(the Boers still speak of Paton's courage),
and so were many men. After the retirement,
the stretcher parties went out, and the Boers
assisted in succouring our wounded, and
behaved on the whole very well, though some
young roughs got out of hand and plundered
the dead and wounded. Their leaders
behaved exceedingly well, and did their best
to restrain them. I went up there and a
more ghastly collection of wounds could not
be imagined, mostly shot at the muzzles of
the rifles in the head, and in some cases with
large Boer bullets. Death must have been
instantaneous. The field cornets told me they
had been expecting the attack, and the
rapidity with which reinforcements arrived—
the presence of General Snyman, and several
leaders, and the destruction of the line,

7

together with the increase of the garrison, tend to endorse their statements. Our wounded were all wounded in front, some of the men retiring backwards so as not to be shot in the back. Sergeant Barry, mortally wounded, sent word to his mother that he had three wounds all in front. Our force was under one hundred actually attacking. The Boers when reinforced about four hundred. Our losses killed or since dead : Captain Vernon, Captain Sandford, Lieutenant Paton, twenty-one rank and file ; wounded : Captain Fitzclarence, twenty-two rank and file; four prisoners. The men retiring were quite cool and willing to have another go—smoking and laughing in some cases, but in the majority bitter and angry at not having got in. British troops have certainly performed as fine feats of arms, but no more determined attack with inferior numbers against an enemy armed with modern rifles in a strong position has ever been pushed home, or a more deliberate and gallant retirement under heavy fire been made. The enemy were much impressed, and said they had never seen such brave men, and though we failed in taking the fort, the action has resulted in the enemy daily strengthening every work, and upset them greatly, as they hourly anticipate a fresh attack, and gusts of musketry break out from their lines at night, for no apparent reason. Indeed, the rapidity with which their white flags were hoisted on the arrival of our ambulances make me, in my own mind, absolutely certain that they were prepared to contemplate surrender, and in any case they will certainly not be able to spare men from this place to assist their retiring commandoes. Altogether their rash and insolent advance into British territory has placed them here, as elsewhere, in about as unpleasant a position for irregular troops as can well be imagined. In the evening we buried our dead.

The Protectorate Regiment, after a life of four months, and a strength of four hundred, has now suffered one hundred and ten casualties. It has accordingly had to be reorganized from four squadrons into three. On no occasion has it been engaged without distinguishing itself, and I think in its last action, though repulsed, it has, if possible, distinguished itself most.

7 *

What I have said about the contemplated surrender of the Boers has since been confirmed by what I heard on my journey south towards Vryburg. Keely, now Resident Magistrate in these parts, had been taken into camp about this time to swear neutrality; and the Boers made no secret of their intention to surrender the fort; but they were kept up to the mark by one determined man, who, lying behind an ammunition box, swore he would blow out the brains of the first man who offered to surrender. It was at this man that Paton was firing through a loophole with a pistol when he was shot. Nobody else on our side seems to have spotted the individual in question, hence the Boers, on our retiring, continued the fight.

27th, 28th, and 29th. Desultory shelling, sniping, and occasional wild firing from the enemy by night. We hear cheering native rumours from the south.

31st, Sunday. Sports, &c., driving competition, horse-show. I won hack competition.

January 1st, 1900, New Year's Day. We had anticipated a quiet day, as this is a Boer festival. I presume they thought we anticipated this, for they commenced early with a heavy bombardment and experimented with incendiary bombs, which however were of no success. A valuable member of the garrison, one of our few carpenters, Slater by name, was killed.

2nd. Our usual shelling, and a niece of a Baralong chief killed in the stadt, amongst others. In the evening Mr. Hamilton, *Times* correspondent, gave the staff and the other correspondents a most excellent dinner, which we all thoroughly appreciated, at Riesle's Hotel. How so good a dinner could be served after about four months' siege is indeed extraordinary.

3rd. The quick Q.-F. Krupp was moved to the north-west of the town, and fired on the western forts, amongst other places into the women's laager, killing two children, one Dutch, one English.

4th. Typhoid has broken out in the women's laager. I suppose we may consider ourselves lucky it is not more prevalent. The usual shelling goes on.

5th. Enemy quiet, with the usual shelling, which is terribly monotonous.

6th.　Boers rather vicious to-day, and the usual Saturday's spar all round at sundown. Runners went north and south.

7th, Sunday.　In the early morning heavy musketry fire from the Boers, quite contrary to their usual custom.　Sports, Christie Minstrels, and a comical turn-out competition.

8th.　Rained hard.　Shelling went on as usual, and my usual sniping ground destroyed by four shells, and the occupant fatally injured. Shrapnell fired over the women's laager.

9th.　From now onwards we may assume a very heavy shelling every day.　Two whites and two natives injured while tampering with a hundred pound shell, one white since dead.

10th.　Mrs. Poulton, born a Dutch woman, shot through the head and killed, also a few natives ; this woman's sister at the commencement of the siege expressed the wish that the streets of Mafeking might run with English blood.　This charming lady, named Hammond, created so much disturbance at the commencement of the siege that she was put under restraint; her daughter has since been severely wounded.　Curses, like chickens, come home to roost.

11th. Usual day of shelling.

12th. A Boer attack on Fort Ayr. They galloped wildly fifty yards in advance of their trenches, about one thousand five hundred yards from Fort Ayr, and indulged in a fantasia, but never came any nearer. Their guns, however, five, twelve, and one hundred pounders, shot very straight and shelled for two hours. Our casualties, one man wounded, since dead.

13th. Big gun did not fire, enemy very quiet ; expect they are running short of small arm ammunition.

14th, Sunday. Great excitement caused by disappearance of Creaky, many rumours. She was seen in at least six different places, but we all hoped she had taken a fond farewell.

15th. Creaky actually discovered about two miles down the Malmani Road. She had apparently been moved by our persistent persecutions, and we thought she had been moved into a worse position for her. We have materially changed our minds, at any rate, at the eastern end of the town, where she fires regularly at meal times, mostly hitting hotels. She commenced firing at 11 o'clock.

16th. Dislike the shelling more since I have fever; one shell struck auxiliary hospital.

17th. Enemy tried to foist Kaffirs into the town, to further diminish our food supply, under a flag of truce. Colonel Baden-Powell refused to receive them. They fired heavily and inexplicably on our white flag carried by Ronny Moncrieffe while retreating. Tremendous indignation in the town, though there is some rumour that one of our Kaffirs fired a shot somewhere (this was subsequently found to be untrue). Shell hit bomb proof occupied by Mr. Vere Stent, Reuter's representative, and myself. Large pieces ricocheted through Dixon's Hotel which was crowded; usual providential escapes.

18th. They shell the town as usual. Most unpleasant this end. They knocked off all corners of the square in two days ; several casualties.

Our system of avoiding the gun is having look-out men in all parts, who ring so many strokes when the gun is loaded, so many when pointed, three strokes for the town, six when pointed off it. The enemy, however, have rather frustrated this, as they do not fire till uncertain intervals after the gun is pointed, ranging from an hour downwards. The lookout then rings another bell, but it gives a remarkably short time to take cover, and it is these odd shells and not a sustained shell fire which causes the loss of life ; at any rate, there is no doubt that since the change of position of the gun a far greater proportion of damage has been done.

19th. There was an artillery duel between one of our seven-pounders—whose shells were made at our own factory here, and the fuses designed by Lieutenant Daniels, B. S. A. P., in which the shells and fuses proved a complete success—and the enemy's five-pounder which was almost immediately silenced. And now as regards the factory. The ammunition for the ship's gun, that weapon of our grandfathers, which was unearthed in the stadt, and which shoots with great violence, though doubtful precision, to enormous ranges, has been cast here. The seven-pounder's shells have been cast, studded, fused, and in every respect made perfect here. Some 2·5-pounder shells, left here by Dr. Jameson, have been fitted with two enlarged driving-bands and have been fired from our seven-pounders with complete success. Too much credit cannot be given to the ingenuity, ability, and energy with which Conolly and all his mates have worked at strengthening that portion of our defences.

20th. The two sides when at trench work happened on each other at night in the vicinity of Fort Ayr, and we drove them back. A very effective day's shelling.

21st, Sunday. Agricultural and produce show, including babies. The first prize for foals since the commencement of the siege to Mr. Minchin, Bechuanaland Rifles; for babies, to Sergeant Brady, B. S. A. P.; a great success, and really extraordinarily good show. My fever nearly gone.

22nd. Rather late shelling to-day, and rumoured attack on Kaffir stadt by Boer friendlies did not take place. A certain amount of firing from Fort Ayr. Rain begun again.

Colonel Baden-Powell protested the other day against the firing on our white flag, and General Snyman, who, as far as I could judge personally whilst in conversation with him after the action at Game Tree fort, is a

crabbed old gentleman, somewhat naturally
rabidly anti-British, and according to the
Boer standard an extreme martinet, sent
in an answer apologising for his burghers
having fired on the white flag, and stating
with regard to Colonel Baden-Powell's remonstrance to his arming and raising the natives,
that he had merely armed a few as cattle
guards. In that case the Boers must have
many cattle in close proximity to our camp,
unseen and unknown to us. He further stated
that he had noticed us building fortifications
on Sunday, to which Colonel Baden-Powell
replied that we had merely taken out and
relaid some mine lines, and that he had been
vastly interested, while riding round the western outposts on Sunday, to see the assiduity
with which the Boers had been working at
their new fortifications in that part.

23rd. The usual sniping continues on the
western front, but peace, punctuated occasionally by one-hundred pound shell, is more or
less prevalent on the eastern. As regards
our food supply, luxuries purchased at store
are a thing of the past, as the authorities have
taken charge of all tinned and other eatables

in the place. We have now stood four months'
siege, and it seems probable that this may be
indefinitely prolonged, and it is mainly owing
to the private enterprise of Mr. Benjamin
Weil, the representative of Julius Weil & Co.
here, that we are really ready to stand, as far
as provisions and stores go, as long a time
again. In addition to having supplied all the
Government required, he laid in large stocks
on his own account, and when the history of
the siege of Mafeking comes to be written, he
will be found to have played by no means the
least important part. In addition to the white
troops employed, and to the Baralongs, who
defend their own stadt, we have four other
black contingents : the Fingoes under Webster,
the Cape Boys under Corporal Currie, C. P.,
a detachment of Baralongs under Sergeant
Abrahams, and the "Black Watch" under
Mackenzie, a mixed Zulu crowd. These
gentry, to their huge delight, are continually
engaged in endeavouring, with some success,
to spend as much gunpowder and spill as
much blood as in them lies. The Cape Boys,
under Corporal Currie, who took charge of
them after Captain Goodyear's wound, from

which I am glad to say he is recovering, have
done notably good service, their motto and
apparently only principle being " Don't know
retiring." In this there is a good deal of
common sense ; for the Boer, though not very
dangerous when faced, becomes deadly and
dangerous when he can shoot quietly at you
as you retire.· There is another portion of our
defences—or perhaps that is a misnomer,
I should rather say of our forces—to which
I have hitherto not alluded, and that is the
excellent transport service. All the mules
were individually selected by Colonel Baden-
Powell and Colonel Walford, assisted by
Mr. Dunlop Smith, A.V.D., and Mr. Mackenzie, transport officer, and anybody who saw the
beautiful spans of mules turned out for the
driving competitions would have felt that in
all cases their choice was well justified, and
the condition of the mules reflected the greatest
credit on the squadron leaders (for each
squadron leader is responsible for his own
transport), conductors and drivers, and to the
care and supervision given by the two officers
before mentioned. The driving was excellent,
and the mules looked in the pink of condition.

Rather heavy shelling, and more sniping than usual. There were several casualties, mostly natives, one shell exploding in a hut and killing and wounding most of its occupants. From this date the authorities have taken over all stores of food and drink, and nothing, even luxuries, can be obtained without an order from headquarters.

24th. Desultory shelling.

25th. There was a good deal of firing to-day round the western trenches. In the evening a native convicted as a spy was executed. He had been sent in to obtain full information as to the stores, forts, their garrisons, and the general disposition of the forces of the town. He quite acknowledged the justice of his sentence, but only seemed to think that it was hard lines that he should be executed before he had had time to procure any information at all. This is the third native spy executed, and the various native contingents are detailed in turn for the duty.

26th. Bradley's Hotel was partially wrecked by a shell. This is the most effective explosion we have so far had. A large piece from the shell went humming overhead beyond the B. S. A. P. fort, quite three-quarters of a mile from its bursting. There is generally time for a morning ride before the big gun commences shelling, but during the last three or four hundred yards into the town, if the bells have begun to ring, there is a certain amount of excitement in returning to the hotel, as it is to this portion of the town that the enemy generally confines his attentions about breakfast time. Later in the afternoon, Lady Sarah Wilson and Captain Wilson, who are both now convalescent, were seated with Major Goold Adams in a passage in the upper storey of the convent, when a shell burst about four feet over their heads, covering them with a pile of bricks and rubbish, but fortunately they escaped with a few bruises. There were rumours of a contemplated attack early next morning, and the northern and western fronts accordingly stood to arms. More significance was given to the rumours in that the Dutch women in the women's laager unanimously sought the shelter of the bomb proofs at an early hour. It was not till the next day that the reason was patent.

27th. During my return from my morning

ride the big gun fired, and I saw the shell burst somewhat short of the women's laager. I naturally supposed this was an accident. It was not, however, the case. The big gun commenced a rapid fire in the same direction, and the effects of the shells as they fell were heliographed back from the western heights. The messages were intercepted by our signallers, under Sergeant Moffat. They placed eight large shells in and close round the laager, and we now understood the reason for the Dutch women taking the cover they did. It was a most deliberate piece of barbarism ; mercifully, there were no casualties.

28th, Sunday. A quiet day. I rode round the western outposts in the morning and found them considerably augmented in strength. They are now a series of bomb-proof block-houses, a zig-zag approach runs from the refugee laager up to Fort Ayr. So approach is possible without danger (which was not so before). A thousand yards to the front of Fort Ayr the new Boer fort is plainly visible, and flies a flag we have not seen before, blue, white, and orange, with a vertical green stripe. It is possible that there may

be some political significance attached to this,
possibly that our friends, the Transvaalers, by
uniting the two Republics, hope to get the
Free State Boers to fight their battles further
away from their own territory ; but, after all,
it is pure surmise, for we get but little news
of any sort—and of political news none at all.
Due south, and about eight hundred yards
away from Fort Ayr, a new fort has been
constructed, commanding the bed of the
Molopo, and garrisoned by Cape Police. It
is about on the position of the old look-out
post. In the afternoon I rode round the
eastern works. A trench now runs from
Ellis's corner across the river, past the gun
emplacement, past Webster's Kraal, up to and
beyond the Nordenfelt position. It is hard to
believe with the much stronger position we
now have, and the reduced number of Boers,
that they will attack again; but, on the other
hand, it is harder to believe that they will
leave Mafeking without a desperate effort to
capture it. In any case, the garrison are
confident. On the termination of evening
service we sing the National Anthem. I have
heard it sung in many places, the most

8

impressive of all at St. Paul's on Jubilee day; certainly next to that occasion, I think the singing of it in Mafeking appealed to me most. For the men who were singing it on Sunday night would be fighting for it on Monday morning. And now, whilst on the subject, and having just read Mr. Kipling's poem, I hope the widows and children of the irregular troops serving out here will not be forgotten when it comes to " pay, pay, pay."

29th. Good news of victories from the south. It seems as if the tide had turned, and as if Old England, slow as usual, was going to forge ahead at last. Her Majesty's message was received with the deepest satisfaction here. It was a month late, but none the less acceptable for being delayed. Colonel Baden-Powell issued an order, in which he referred to the execution of the spy, and warning all persons, women included, who might be found treasonably corresponding with the enemy, that, on conviction, they would be inevitably shot; also that he regretted having to take such strong measures, but that as the enemy chose to fire on the women's laager, he should confine the Dutch

THE OLD NAVAL GUN AT WORK.

prisoners in a gaol constructed in the laager, so that, if the enemy persisted in their brutality, they would kill their own friends. (It was a curious coincidence that on Sunday, after Saturday's performance, there was a feeling of insecurity in the town, and most people were of opinion that in all probability the Boers would violate the Sunday. truce; but when the Dutch women were seen walking about, the feeling of confidence was quickly restored.) In the afternoon the gun bequeathed to us by Lord Nelson commenced firing on the Boer laager at Wessel's Springs, near the head of the waterworks—a range of something over three thousand yards. Her round shot bounded about the veldt through, over, short of, the laager, rapidly dispersing a mounted body of Boers in its proximity; for, unlike a shell, when she strikes, you have by no means done with her. The drill is somewhat complicated, but thanks to an edition of Captain Marryatt's works, we have succeeded in resuscitating this long extinct form of exercise.

30th. The results of our ancient piece's firing last night has been that the laager has

shifted away, in the direction of Signal Hill,
and that the Boers generally have been so
busy that they have not yet found time (mid-
day) to discharge their Creuzot gun.   There
was an alarm last night, and the eastern
front and reserve squadron were held in
readiness all night.   Yesterday the Boers
re-established themselves on the nearest brick-
kiln, and a sniping entertainment was organized for them by Corporal Currie, C. P., who
has charge of the Cape Boy Post, within three
hundred yards.   One Boer, who for some
extraordinary reason, wore a white shirt
(which he will never do again) occasionally
showed his back over the edge of a shelter he
was constructing for himself, acting apparently on the principle of the ostrich,
Trooper Piper of the Cape Police eventually
got him, and at the same moment, his friend
who was firing from a loop-hole, fired at
Piper ; fortunately Currie, who was covering
the loop-hole, fired almost simultaneously and
got him too, to the huge delight of the Cape
Boys ; stretchers came up under the Red
Cross and removed the bodies, the second
man was a bearded man and a well known

sniper, he was an excellent shot, and the news of his demise was received with universal pleasure by the garrison, while for the rest of the day his friends made the post very warm for its occupants.

31st. There is one effect of this continual shell fire which is perhaps undesirable, and that is the remarkable degree of selfishness it engenders. There is really nothing to do and no excitement. News is rare, and not always of the best, and with lack of the proper amount of exercise and the frequent ringing of bells, which are almost as bad as the shells themselves, tempers get short, and the solicitude on " No. 1's " account increases. However, entertainments like the one organized this evening, go far to relieve our spleen and vary the interminable monotony of the siege. We were warned in the afternoon that our artillery was going to bombard the Boer lines, and from various points of vantage numerous spectators strolled out to look on. Personally, I made my way to the trench running from Ellis's corner to the river, and selected a spot where I was well away from other people, and which commanded a good view of the

Boer trench, and, above all, of the big gun,
which showed clearly against the white
marquees in rear of it. At the time there was
no firing going on, and cattle on both sides
were being brought home. Absolute stillness
reigned, only broken by the lowing of the
beasts, the sounds of the poultry yards, and
the barking of dogs. These, with the drowsy
hum of the insects, made one feel extremely
sleepy, and one might well have imagined
oneself lolling between two peaceful villages
at home. However, at 5.30 p.m. a change
came very distinctly " o'er the spirit of the
dream." Our guns commenced, three seven-
pounders and the Nordenfeldt, and steadily
shelled for about an hour, answered by the
nine-pounder quick-firer, five-pounder Krupps,
and old Creaky, who swung her nose backwards and forwards from one extremity of
the eastern defences to the other, making, on
the whole, moderate but extremely varied
practice, As I had a pair of very strong
glasses, a small cluster soon collected around
me, thereby inviting the undesirable attentions
of their riflemen, who, however, were pretty
well engaged themselves, and consequently

did not annoy us very much. It was about
as safe a performance for the onlookers as
could well be imagined. The guns drew
most of the fire, and were scattered over
a large extent of front. One could plainly
see the big gun, and when she fired our way,
had ample time to get into the trench. There
were no casualties on our side, but after dark
the Boers, who had been much upset by
this disturbance of their reliefs and feeding
arrangements, commenced to shell the town,
killing one man outside the newspaper offices,
and contriving, in some extraordinary manner,
to drop a fragment of shell down the chimney of
the headquarters' staff offices. This they continued till past nine, doing no further damage,
except to houses. The Boers in the course
of the day put a five-pounder shell through
a portion of the hospital, and at night fired
a volley into the operating room, where
a patient was being examined. So we conclude that they must have lost some men
during the day, which made them vicious.
During the past fortnight they fired upon
a flag of truce, deliberately shelled the
women's laager, and fired on the hospital.

February 1st. To-day completes the six-
teenth week of the siege, and we have had
plenty of shell fire to celebrate it; one big
shell, I regret to say, bursting on a splinter
proof at Cannon Kopje, wrecking it, and
killing one man and wounding two others.
These splinter proofs were a line of trenches
running down towards the town from the
kopje, and it had seemed that by no chance
could they possibly be struck direct by
a shell.   In the evening the Boer shell fire
again continued till a late hour, and the last
explosion that we heard puzzled us a good
deal.   It subsequently transpired that Major
Panzera and Corporal Currie, with three
natives, had crept up to the nearest brick-
kiln, from which the Boers were unfortunately
absent, and had blown it up with fifty pounds
of dynamite.   This will probably keep the
Boers away from that locality for a while, as
they are not unnaturally very cautious of
approaching any place where they suspect
the presence of dynamite.   A Kimberley
native informed us that they stop the natives
going home from the Kimberley mines and
ask them if there is dynamite laid down

round the town, to which the natives generally reply, "Plenty!" They seem to be
having a much better time in Kimberley
than we are here, as the natives say we
live here like mere cats, whilst they have
apparently no big gun to annoy them down
there.

2nd. They began shelling later here to-day,
so one's morning's ride was uninterrupted,
but they are, however, now in full swing
again. Sergeant Francis, B. S. A. P., died of
wounds received at Cannon Kopje. Our
usual shelling.

3rd. We sent off runners north and
south. In the morning the enemy devoted
his attention to the town. But in the
afternoon our seven-pounder and Nordenfeldt, east of Cannon Kopje, commenced
firing on the enemy, who were constructing
a new trench, considerably in advance of the
old position of the big gun on the S.E.
heights. Consequently Creaky vigorously
assailed them in turn, and the Krupp gun
and the one-pound Maxim galloped from
McMullen's farm to her assistance. The big
gun made very good shooting, but fortunately

only one man was hit, and he by a sand-bag
hurled up by a shell aimed at the Nordenfeldt. The Nordenfeldt gun detachment
consists of two men, Privates Lowe and
Mulholland, both of the Railway Volunteers,
and these two men have served this gun
for months daily, often under a heavy fire
directed entirely at them. At the same time
our beloved relic of Lord Nelson was
engaged on the western front in bombarding
the new fort in front of Fort Ayr, being
answered on that front and assisted by
musketry and rifle fire. The week, as usual,
culminated in the customary Saturday evening flare-up all round. The big gun was
cleaned and oiled for Sunday, and we thought
it was all over till Monday morning. This,
however, was not the case. The Boers were
unusually jumpy. They treated us to incendiary shells till late, and kept up a heavy
musketry fire at fitful intervals during the
night. They commenced constructing a new
trench in the Brickfields, and can plainly be
heard working at it.

4th, Sunday. The usual quiet day.
At Fort Ayr, while cleaning the Maxim,

it was accidentally discharged, and the
Boers promptly answered, so Mr. Greenfield, in charge of the post, strolled out to
explain matters, and was met half way by the
Boer representatives, who talked to him for
a bit, gave him the latest news (presumably
untrue), exchanged little harmless chaff, and
agreed to swap newspapers for whisky.
The newspapers, needless to say, contained
flaming accounts of universal Boer victories,
which, here, one finds it somewhat hard to
credit, and they agreed to furnish similar
papers next Sunday. It is curious to see in
the advertisement sheets advertisements from
manufacturers, stating themselves to be
manufacturers to Her Majesty the Queen,
to read the London letter, and a column of
society chit-chat in a paper published in the
capital of our enemy. However, it is an odd
world.

5th. Two lots of runners came in
from the north this morning. Personally,
I received my first communication from
home since the siege began, only a wire
though. Quite a number of letters came in,
but were very unequally distributed. One

receiving a dozen, the vast majority none.
Hanbury Tracey was exceptionally fortunate,
as he received a money-lender's circular and
a bill, re-addressed in red ink, from his
orderly room at home, and that was his sole
communication. They shelled us as usual,
and kept it up late. A wet night, but that
did not seem to deter them. Their incendiary shells were, as usual, a failure.

6th. Shelling all day, and firing at night.
Two natives were killed and Colonel Hore,
commanding Protectorate Regiment, had
a narrow escape whilst returning from
the Court of Summary Jurisdiction.

7th. They commenced shelling early
this morning, so far with little damage.
There seem regular streaks of luck in
this shell fire, and sometimes we strike
a very bad one, but it is really marvellous
how these huge shells have done comparatively little injury to life here. From what
we can gather from other places, it will be
about the worst knocked about town in South
Africa. The remains of some buildings have
been removed and the majority will require
re-building. Yesterday, a shell went clean

through the smoke box and boiler of a
locomotive, and did not explode until striking
the ground beyond. One also pitched on the
top of an unfortunate native in an engine ash-
pit and destroyed him. The price of food has
naturally risen enormously and will probably
rise more. The humble Kaffir, if he possesses
a hen which lays regularly, can maintain himself and another. An egg fetches sixpence, and
a Kaffir's ration of mealie meal only comes to
threepence sterling, consequently the henless
Kaffir sponges upon his more wealthy brother.

This afternoon I rode up to Cannon Kopje
and arrived simultaneously with a ninety-four
pound shell from the contrary direction. We
did not, however, hurt each other, and I dismounted and tethered my horse under the
best cover available, and to ground with me
like a rabbit. They fired one or two more
shells at the kopje, doing no harm, and we
then strolled up to the look-out post to have
a look at our persecutor. It was a lovely
evening, and as she was then pointed on the
town, one could view her proceedings with
the utmost equanimity, speculating mildly
as to whether she would pitch her shell on

one's own bomb proof or not. The shell,
however, burst prematurely, just clear of the
muzzle of the gun, and we continued watching
the town and the rest of the defences, all of
which lie like a panorama from the Cannon
Kopje look-out. Creaky was then re-loaded,
and with her nose cocked high in the air, was
apparently aimed in the direction of the planet
Venus. As a matter of fact, however, she was
aimed at Fort Ayr, and after the discharge
one imagined one could trace the projectile in
its flight by the hurtling sound it made ; but
when by sound it seemed as far as Fort
Miller, one could see the strike close by Fort
Ayr (which is about four miles from the
gun), and yet the noise of the projectile
through the air continued for some seconds
longer, producing a very curious effect. She
re-loaded and was again pointed on the town
when slowly she swung her nose round and
was pointed on *us*, a roar of look out from
the man on duty, and the crowd of languid
spectators was transformed into a body of
active men, heading straight for their
accustomed shelters, which having attained,
they peered carefully at the gun, waiting for

the smoke from the muzzle, which would be
the signal for their final disappearance. We
waited and waited, but she came not, so,
deciding that it was the good-night gun,
I walked back, accompanied by one of the
garrison of the kopje, and ate my dinner at the
hotel with the comforting assurance that
I had last seen her directed a good mile from
the dining-room.

This morning Corporal Currie and his
men killed and wounded a few Boers,
coming at dawn to their trenches. The
Boers consequently gave us a quiet day, as
their obsequies and attendant ceremonies
seemed to fill in all their time; but at dark
they commenced a heavy fire of small arms,
shell, and vituperation, upon our advanced
post, about two hundred and fifty yards from
their main trench. They assure the garrison
of this post that they intend to make it
particularly warm for them, and it is about
as warm a corner as one could well select.
I rode out in the afternoon to Captain
Marsh's post on the western edge of the
stadt, we have there driven the Boers out of
and occupied Fort Cronje, a mile from the

western edge, and seven hundred yards from
the nearest Boer fort. This Fort Cronje
commands the whole of the valley on the
other side of the ridge, under cover of which
the Boers used to remove their reliefs and
reinforcements to and from Cronje's laager
and the western laager. Its capture has
largely extended our field for grazing. We
had proposed to walk out there, but on
consultation we decided not to, as one is
under a pretty heavy fire in the open the last
part of the journey, and one would see it
better and under more favourable circumstances on the Sunday, during the truce.
Riding back, I tried a short cut, at a good
pace; the Boers, however, were not quite
asleep, and began sniping with marvellous ill-
success, as I was about to get under cover
again. To-day we were informed that we
must be prepared to hold out for another four
months, which we are quite ready to do.
The garrison and inhabitants received the
intelligence with the utmost equanimity felt
no earthly doubt as to the result, merely expressing extreme boredom at the prospect of
four months more of such monotonous existence.

9th. A runner from the south arrived, informing us of Buller's crossing the Tugela. Comparing this news with the Boer accounts of British defeats with heavy losses on the 24th, south of Tugela, one can only conclude that they must indeed be in a bad plight when they can invent such amazingly circumstantial and appalling lies. However, I hope we are nearing the end of the last act, and "God Save the Queen." They have been quiet to-day, and as far as we know, no funerals to occupy them so hope and trust that they are digesting some bad news ; the Kaffir who brought the messages states that the Free Staters have had enough of it, but that Cronje will not allow them to surrender, as they had everything to lose and absolutely nothing to gain ; we can well believe it. The Kimberley correspondence is of a chatty description, refers to the weather and papers (which have not arrived), but the gist of the whole is cheerful and consequently welcome, though we should prefer news. Their food supply seems good, which is consoling. But this much is certain, that if we have to hold out another four

months, the means of our doing so, in the
supply line, is due to the presence of Mr. B.
Weil. I wonder whether it is appreciated,
even yet at home, what a stupendous and
monumental liar the Boer is. The Kaffir says
what he thinks you will like. The Boer,
however, says what he knows he likes himself.
I hope some day to read a British account of
the war. The Boer account would pain me if
I believed it.

10th. The enemy remained quiet, at
least as regards their big gun, yesterday evening, though the now nightly
fusillade began about 8 o'clock. This
morning they commenced shelling late, and
apparently directed their projectiles at the
Mill, which works every night, protected by a
traverse, at the south-eastern corner of the
town. They only fired two projectiles, one of
which struck Mr. J. Dall, Town Councillor,
and commander of one of the Town Guard
posts, full, blowing him to pieces. His wife,
poor woman, who was in the women's laager,
where the intelligence was abruptly conveyed
by a panic stricken Kaffir woman servant,
came up semi-distracted, under the escort of

the Rev. W. H. Weekes. It was, of course, impossible that she should see him, and the scene was a very painful one for her friends in their endeavours to be of some comfort to her. Musketry and the discharge of field pieces continued all the afternoon, during which we had an exceedingly heavy thunderstorm which flooded some of the uncompleted and advanced trenches, compelling the evacuation of the one within two hundred yards of the Boer main trench, during which operation—one of our men was wounded. The others remained there, and sought the best cover from fire they could in its immediate propinquity. Firing continued all round the outposts, at intervals all night and well into the dawn on Sunday morning. Since we have been warned to be ready for four months more siege, the question of food supplies for natives has become very serious. Two of these unfortunate fugitives were shot last night in their endeavours to elude the vigilance of the cordon all round us. It is not the question of meat so much as the question of grain, which is our difficulty.

11th, Sunday. I was aroused about

dawn by musketry fire, and as I heard no more, supposed I had been dreaming, but when starting for my early ride, was told there had been heavy firing to the east. I went to Fort Ayr, from whence the Boer fort seemed ridiculously close, and so on to the Cape Police fort, and from there the Boer sniping station looked within six hundred yards. I was, however, informed that it was a good sixteen hundred yards off. It was a perfectly lovely morning, and had one's horse only felt as fresh as the morning, the ride would have been indeed enjoyable, but the stress of the siege in the way of shortness of provisions has fallen far more severely on the horses than the human beings. From this fort I rode to the B. Squadron horse lines. The horses are not at present a pleasing spectacle, but, owing to our extended grazing ground, I dare say they could still do some work. Sundry of them are killed and turned into billtong for the Kaffirs. Thence along the picturesque bank of the Molopo, through the centre of the stadt to breakfast at Captain Marsh's. This officer, whose squadron has held the stadt

since the commencement of the siege, has, from
his West Coast experiences, a wonderful knack
of dealing with natives, and in a great measure
the absolute confidence of the Baralongs in
the white garrison may be ascribed to him, they
have accordingly constituted him a sort of
universal referee in all their local troubles.
After breakfast we walked out from the edge of
the stadt to the two forts occupied by Sergeant
Abrahams and his detachment of natives, within
six hundred yards of which are situated
the Boer forts, also garrisoned by natives.
Between the opposing forts both sides rambled
at their own sweet will. We then went on to
Fort Cronje, originally in the occupation of
the Boers, and having attained our utmost
limits we sat and smoked and looked at the
stadt (distant about a mile), and appreciated
how Mafeking looked to the Boers from their
western outposts. Personally, the northern
end of the stadt reminds me of nothing so
much as the Curragh Camp when viewed from
the Newbridge Road, and, indeed, the veldt
all round looked fresh, green, and undulating
enough for the Curragh itself. Fort Cronje
is enfiladed by the blockhouse north of the

Molopo. Eastward from Sergeant Abrahams'
fort, and in a circular direction across the
railway line towards Cannon Kopje, extend
forts occupied by McKenzie's contingent.
We thus now have a large and secure grazing
ground, the area of which I had not previously
appreciated. We strolled back to the stadt and
rode back to shop and church. During the
morning and afternoon occurred some of
those interchanges of courtesy between ourselves and our opponents, which generally do
take place on Sunday. Corporal Currie, who
during the week spends all his time in endeavouring to slay and not be slain by the Boers,
was called over by them to translate a note
they had received. They offered him tobacco
and small civilities, and patted him on the back
saying he was a "freundlish kerel." They
also said they were sick of it, and what a
waste of time it was not to be ploughing. A
somewhat similar conversation was carried
on by Mr. Greenfield on the other side.
The Dutch, in addition, said they thought it
would all be over in a month, that they
hadn't got any papers, but would give them to
us at the first opportunity, which we under-

stood to mean, when their romancing jour-
nalists had sufficiently seasoned the dish of
Dutch defeats for Mafeking consumption.
The bicycle sports had to be postponed owing
to the condition of the track, but there was a
cricket match in the morning between Fitzclarence's squadron and the town of Mafeking,
which the latter won by nineteen runs, and in
the afternoon a concert, where our commanding officer, as usual, distinguished himself by
his comic songs and humourous sketches.
This talent is well known to his friends, but
is certainly not so well known to the British
public, who only have had the advantage of
viewing him from a serious side ; however, we
appreciated him quite as much in his lighter
capacity, and the concert was a great success.
The Beleagured Batchelors' Ball, given by the
batchelors of Mafeking, had in consequence of
Mr. Dall's death been postponed till to-night.
It commenced merrily enough, and had been
going on for about an hour when history and
the Duchess of Richmond's ball repeated
itself. The staff officer arrived warning all
officers to fall in. Heavy firing commenced
all round, and an attack was anticipated. The

galloping Maxim raced across the veldt in the
dark from the westen outposts to the town, at
no time a pleasant journey, and now with the
innumerable pitfalls all round it, it was lucky
to get there without a smash. The Bechuanaland Rifles and a squadron of the Protectorate
Regiment were pushed forwards towards the
brickfields, taking the place of the Cape Police
who had reinforced the extreme eastern advanced posts. The Boers had put three
hundred more men into their advance trench
and kept up a heavy fire at intervals all night,
as indeed they did at all points. Our men
did not fire much.

12th. At dawn this morning I went
to Ellis's corner, as heavy firing was
going on in that direction. The five-
pounder was firing at Currie's post and the
Cape Police, from the Boer main trench at
under two hundred yards. Their quick firer
and one-pound Maxim were also doing so.
The big gun seemed anxious to participate,
and was elevated several times, but owing to
the Boer trench being immediately in the
line of fire did not venture to. Things
slackened somewhat at half-past six, and I

IN THE TRENCHES.

By permission of "The Daily Graphic."

went for a ride round the western side where a few odd shots were being fired, but nothing was going on. About half-past eight the big gun commenced firing at Cannon Kopje, and after half a dozen shots transferred her attentions to the town, mainly bursting in fairly close proximity to this dug-out, but so far no damage to my knowledge. This afternoon I take up my residence at Cannon Kopje for a bit.

12th. When I had finished the last paragraph I left my dug-out and went to lunch, and as I walked to the hotel, heard a single shot, of which I naturally took no notice. An hour afterwards I heard that it had claimed its victim in Captain R. Girdwood, late 3rd Battalion Royal Irish Rifles, assistant commisariat officer here, who was mortally wounded. To the garrison and all who knew him the blow was severe. Throughout the whole siege he was always laughing and joking, and nothing ever subdued his never-failing cheerfulness : to meet him was a regular tonic if liver or temper were at fault. The duty he did in assisting Captain Ryan to regulate the supplies of food and stores was invaluable, and

Colonel Baden-Powell in his general order literally expressed the great regret and sympathy felt for his wife. In the evening I went up to the kopje, and am for a time attached to the B. S. A. P. Prior to my departure they gave us a good doing in the town, both musketry and shell fire.

13th. To sleep in the open and live on the heights in fine weather is undoubtedly an improvement on the town, at any rate for a short time ; though one is away from headquarters and the latest garrison gossip, one's view of proceedings is universal and uninterrupted, unless one happens to be the recipient of Boer favours. The bomb proof gives ample cover and a dining-room, for the rest one lives in the open which, in this perfect weather, unless the sun be unduly hot, is charming, and though washing arrangements be scanty, the air is better and the view far less circumscribed than in the town some two thousand yards away. Last night wild musketry fire went on all night, and incendiary Boer shells provided the kopje contingent with fireworks gratis, and only succeeded in setting one house on fire, which

was quickly extinguished. Poor Girdwood
died this afternoon and was buried this
evening.

14th, Valentine's Day. I rode into the
town and having transacted my business,
and had a pleasant ride round the western
outposts, returned just in time to elude
their first shells. They are messing about
their works as usual, but what they are
doing we cannot quite make out. They have,
however, withdrawn their marquees from
their gun at McMullan's farm. The homely
Dutch families generally play about the gun
(the Asp on the Cocktrice's den—N.B. the
Cocktrice's business end directed on us), and
when family life is most in evidence in the
gun's vicinity they generally fire on the town,
as it does not amuse the dear things to fire at
a small mark where they may possibly do no
damage, whilst they think they cannot well
miss everybody in the town. The fair ladies
frequently fire the gun themselves and dandle
their babies on high to look on at the prospec-
tive slaughter of English women and children.
Charming race! I think even Sheridan could
scarcely find a Dutch woman " an excuse for

a glass," or, indeed, an excuse for anything else. However, if their menkind had as much pluck as they possess venom, Mafeking would not now be flying the Union Jack, but the Vierkleur of bilious hue. This is plentiful in the vicinity, but has not, and will not, desecrate the township, and I trust the new issue may serve as a model for the ribbon of our Transvaal medal. Sundown: Creaky dismantled. Are they sick of it at last?

15th. As dawn broke a crowd of us went up to the lookout post, to look for our dear departed, and when we failed to find her we accepted our loss with due philosophy. I rode over to Fort Ayr to see Mr. Greenfield, who is isolated for a month in this post. He must, when not engaged in rallies with the Boers, find it very dull, for he accepted with avidity the offer of my diary of the siege to read. He had, however, found Creaky in front of his position and about five miles due west of the town; what she proposes to do here time will show, but our end is pretty safe from her. Later I received a telephone message to say how pleased he was with the account of the fight of November 31st. This blunder, in my diary, is a legacy from my late typewriter. His last batch of copy (which was the last straw that gave the correspondent the " hump ") dated the 12th, though irritating, was rather amusing, I have now transferred my favours elsewhere. The gun has commenced bombarding the stadt and women's laager.

16th. I rode up to Major Godley's and had the " 31st of November " cast in my teeth once more (since corrected). The big gun fired twenty-eight shots at the stadt and women's laager. From Cannon Kopje there is twenty-three-and-a-half seconds between the smoke from her muzzle and the report, which makes her a matter of nine thousand yards away, and about the same from the centre of the town which she cannot now properly reach, and to strike which at all, she is elevated apparently at right angles. She devoted several shells to McKenzie's western shelter trenches, doing no harm, however. Her change of position must have been another deliberate atrocity on the part of the Boers, for which I trust their Commander will be strictly called to account. There can be no immediate effect expected on

10

the defences or ultimate resistance of Mafeking
by the deliberate bombardment of women and
children, black or white. And he who sows
the storm may reap the whirlwind, for the
blacks neither forget nor forgive, and this is
one more, and by no means the least, tally in
a long score. Now, as regards the position of
the Baralongs and our other native residents.

At the outbreak of the war, the Boers
flooded the town with all the refugee Kaffirs
from Johannesburg and other parts of the
Transvaal, who happened to be in our vicinity,
hoping either on the capture of the town,
which they confidently anticipated, to secure
a good labour market, or, in the event of an
unexpectedly protracted resistance, to exercise
through these additional mouths, a severe
pressure on our food supplies, and thus
indirectly on our length of defence. They
carefully, however, first robbed them of all
their money. Now, picking a Kaffir's pocket,
or wherever he may carry his money, ranks
about as high in the code of honour, as
stealing coppers from a blind man's plate.
I am not sure whether it is a transgression of
the Law of Nations, but as by the time this

diary is read the Boer will not be, as he certainly never ought to have been, a nation, it is of small moment, but the act of robbery distinctly took place. The Baralongs were assured by both sides that the war was between two white races, and that they had no cause to interfere. We went even further, and refused to allow them to assist us. However, when the Baralong had seen his cattle raided, his kraals burnt, and himself bombarded, he, somewhat of a rhetorician, but lacking perhaps in the logical capacity for distinguishing between "a military operation" and "an act of war," decided that the Boers' application of the former to his property was good enough excuse for him to indulge in the latter to prevent a further application, he accordingly, in his childlike manner, invited the Boers to enter his stadt, and shot several of them when they tried to. Recently, too, the Boers made overtures to secure the Baralong assistance, and the Chief, Wessels, said he must think it over; after long deliberation he declined. It was probably in order to punish them for this lack of readiness to support them, that

10 *

the Boers so slated the stadt. However this may be, the Baralongs and other natives have loyally and consistently supported us, and deserve ample compensation for the hardships, privations, and losses which they have sustained. All day the Boers have been making feeble attempts on McKenzie's outpost ; and at night, seated at the kopje, one could see a circle of fire running all round the outposts. On the eastern side, our Maxim in the brickfields, our seven-pounder and their five-pounder and many rifles were flashing in the darkness ; in the distance Fort Ayr was warmly engaged, while to support McKenzie in our immediate proximity, the armoured train was creaking and groaning up the grass-grown line. And nothing perhaps brings home our isolation so much, as to see the rails overgrown with grass, and reflect that this is a main line to England. Owing to the custom of the Boer of elevating the muzzle of his rifle over the parapet and firing in the air, bullets were whistling and falling all round us on the kopje all night, which, as we were a mile from, and two hundred feet higher than, the trench they were firing at, argued poor marksmanship on their part. However, we were all fairly safe, and the Boer presumably quite so, and as he made plenty of noise I suppose everybody was satisfied.

17th. Very little firing till the evening, and then usual performance.

18th, Sunday. Our usual quiet day. The bank now opens for business on Sundays. As the Kaffirs, in common with other natives, persist in burying their specie, it is very literally locked up, and to restore the circulation of silver we have a paper issue for small sums. Indeed, we are now a very self-contained community, we have our bank, our ordnance factory, our police, and flourish under a beneficent and remote autocracy. As regards the ordnance, the factory was started for the manufacture of shells for our seven-pounders, for shot, brass and iron, for our antique cannon, and for the adaptation of five-pounder shells (left here by Dr. Jameson) to our seven-pounders by the addition of enlarged driving bands; these have all proved a complete success, and too much praise cannot be given to Connely and Cloughlan of the Locomotive Department, who have organized and run the aforesaid factory. As great a triumph has been the manufacture of powder, and invention of fuses by Lieutenant Daniel, B. S. A. P., and Glamorgan Artillery Militia, and thus we are rendered secure against our ammunition running short; a gun is also being manufactured, and will shortly be used. This factory is of long standing, but prior to this the authorities have not allowed us to allude to its existence.

19th. Went out to try and shoot plover, which form an acceptable addition to our rations, as we have now come down to horse-flesh and six ounces of bread per day. Fairly quiet day. Strolling down to town in the evening, I assumed that their snipers were too much occupied with our people in the brickfields to bother about me. They were not, however, and were unpleasantly attentive.

20th. Re-transferred my residence to the town, the firing is heavier down here through the day, and also, indeed, the night, but here we are under cover.

21st. Gun did not fire more than two or three shots, but at night there was very heavy firing along the brickfield front, they shot some of the working party, and also headed some of the natives going towards Kanya. The Boers made a half-hearted sort of attempt to turn our men out of the advanced trench, but utterly failed. The question of feeding the natives has been solved by the establishment of a soup kitchen, the component parts of the stock may be varied, but the result is eminently nutritious.

Gun changed back near to old position east of town, they elevated and depressed her several times, but did not fire. As the bells rung, however, the moral effect was exactly the same, possibly also the physical. Sergeant-Major Looney, A. S. C., was reduced to the ranks and five years penal servitude awarded to him for selling Government stores. Private Miller, Protectorate Regiment, tampering with a loaded ninety-four-pound shell, was blown to pieces. This form of lunacy is apparently ineradicable. We anticipate an attack to-morrow, as it is the Orange Free State Independence Day. I wonder if the Free State still exists : the following letter *apropos* of this from the leader of the opposition in the Free State before the war is, I think, interesting :—

(*Copy.*)

BLOMFONTEIN,
September 4th, 1899.

CHARLES METTAM, ESQ.,
Box 23.
Krugersdorp.

DEAR MR. METTAM,

Your letter of the 30th inst. is to hand, and affords a by no means solitary instance of the one sided and high-handed treatment former Free State Burghers have to undergo at the hands of our so-called brethren in the South African Republic, yet in spite of all this the political union or alliance was put through our Raad, and should hostilities break out, we shall have to be belligerants and be involved in all the horrors of war and have to lose our independence, and for what? As a just reward for the folly of allowing a spurious sentiment to override common sense. So it is, however—and under the circumstances, as you have lost your Free State burgher rights you could not claim protection here. The only way I see for you—as you hold to your birthright staters—is to bring your position to the notice of the British resident, and ask him to advise you how you are to act. With kindest regards to Mrs. Mettam and yourself.

Yours faithfully,
J. G. FRASER.

P.S.—I think a great many of our people are being

educated by this crisis to the accuracy of the policy which I placed before them at the last election, and have since always advocated.

J. G. F.

HER MAJESTY'S AGENCY,

PRETORIA,

September 11th, 1899.

SIR,

I beg to acknowledge receipt of your letter and enclosure (herewith returned) of the 7th instant, and regret that it is not in my power to discuss the matter to which you refer by letter. I should, however, recommend you, if you should be in Johannesburg, to see the British Vice-Consul there, who will no doubt give you such advice as may be possible under the circumstances.

I am, Sir,

Your obedient servant,

CONYNGHAM GREENE.

MR. C. METTAM,

    P. O. Box 23,

        Krugersdorp.

Certified true copy.

E. H. CECIL MAJ,

C. S. O.

23rd. They commenced shelling cattle and northern end of the town. As the inhabitants have not been shelled severely for ten days, they seem more concerned in running to see where the shell pitches, than in taking cover as they have been strictly warned to do. Steady rain has commenced, depressing the big gun and the Boers.

24th. Rain continuing, gun and owners still depressed. No news received for ten days and great universal anxiety felt for anticipated decisive intelligence.

25th, Sunday. No heavy shelling yesterday, but firing all night and this morning. Cape Boys in advanced trenches, and Boers, engaged in an argument as to their respective mothers and other female relatives' merits and demerits. The arguments for and against having rapidly degenerated to assertions, shooting began, but as it was merely a personal quarrel no one else interfered, and, indeed, white flags from both sides met within a quarter of a mile of the firing, which continued all day. Our Sunday concert was a great success, and the day being fine was most enjoyable. It is curious what different people buy at the stores, the Europeans buying mainly the necessities of life, while the Kaffir, who has plenty of money, but is only allowed to purchase a limited amount of meal, browses off Pâte de Foie Gras, and other similar comestibles. In the afternoon I went to inspect our new gun. She reflects the greatest credit on her builders, the finish and turn-out being quite dandy. She's a smooth bore 5·5, and carries a round shell ; we ought to have good fun from her.

26th. Runners in this morning, news very meagre. Her Majesty's telegram received, which gave intense satisfaction, but we have been anxiously anticipating decisive intelligence. The Kaffirs report that the Boers are few round here, but will not abandon the prosecution of the siege; on our side we cannot afford a serious sortie, as a reverse *might* mean the fall of Mafeking, which is not desirable or in the least probable. The Boers began shell-fire at dawn this morning, and continued it at intervals all day. This was the most rapid fire we have had, and the continuous clanging of bells might have induced a stranger to suppose that we were indulging in some popular celebration. They particularly favoured our end of the town. In the evening we tried our new gun on Game Tree fort at about 2300 yards, she was a great success, and her range was apparently only limited by eyesight.

27th. Being Majuba Day we expected an attack, so I went up to Cannon Kopje before dawn. What attacking there was was in the brickfields and was done by us, but after a fitful splutter of musketry for an hour things quieted down. I went up to Fort Ayr but nothing was doing, and with the exception of musketry fire and a few small shells, it was a quiet day. The Boers blew up the line about two miles north of the town.

28th. We have got our news at last, and though the shell fire is very much heavier than usual the population is wandering about with a bland smile on its face and a comfortable contempt for the Boer nation at large, only tempered by the fear that the military success over Boer armies in the field may be discounted greatly if the British people allow themselves to be hoodwinked by the most unscrupulous, self-interested politicians who ever led a country to its ruin, but who have unfortunately sown seeds which may sprout again and to which there is only one successful treatment, that of

force majeure, followed by *pax Brittanica*,
to be upheld again whenever necessary by
the aforesaid *force majeure*, which is the
only argument that South Africa, black or
white, in its present condition can understand. Generosity would be wasted, kindness
treated with ill-concealed contempt, and blood
and treasure cast away, whilst race hatred
would again be rampant, were the Dutch
to be once more in a position to struggle for
supreme control. It is a strong man armed who
keeps South Africa, let that man be British.

The Boers are determined to keep us
amused, and do not approve of the Free
Press ; they have just now blown the newspaper office, by our dug-out, to pieces, and are
trying to silence our mild manifestations of
joy by particularly heavy shell fire. This
afternoon we tried our new gun again on
the veldt, with bursting charges in the shells,
and the results were eminently satisfactory;
they afforded a certain amount of interest to
the garrison of Game Tree fort, who, as the
gun was pointed almost at right angles to
them, bobbed somewhat unnecessarily to each
discharge. The explosion of the shell might

well have puzzled them for it was exactly
like the discharge of another gun. It is a
shame to be cooped up here in such weather,
" where all around is beautiful and only Boers
are vile," and if they had any sense of
decency or humour they would give us one
good fight to finish, as it is we hang on in
trenches into which they cannot possibly
come, they hang on in opposing trenches into
which we cannot afford to go, exchanges of
shots go on all day, varied by shell fire on
their part, which is becoming monotonous,
and the dullest, deadest level of warfare has
been effectually attained. To-day we had
our little joke ; a dummy truck was placed on
the line about two miles south of the town,
some snipers fired a few shots from it and
then abandoned it, they were, however, successful in drawing the fire from the quick-
firer Krupp and one-pound Maxim at Jackal
Tree with occasional shots from the big gun ;
they made execrable shooting, but killed
some cattle and a horse or two in a remote
portion of the veldt, and unfortunately killed
the Sergeant-Major of the Black Watch, a
fine Zulu over six feet four inches: a one-

pound Maxim hit him clean in the head. Yesterday, too, Trooper Elkington, a particularly smart, good-looking fellow in the Cape Police, was struck in the face by a five-pound shell, and his nose and eyes destroyed ; he still lives, poor fellow. *Apropos* of Zulus, there is a mad Zulu in the town who, when the frenzy seizes him, strips, and indulges in a war dance in front of the Boers ; how many thousand rounds of ammunition they have fired at him it would be hard to say, but one day for certain they fired a five nine-pounder Krupp at him, the only result being that he assegaied the spot were each shell fell. My own personal experience of him was aggravating. One day having selected a secluded spot with good cover from which to snipe, and thinking myself exceedingly well concealed, I was much annoyed by the inordinate amount of bullets which came my way, and whilst waiting till they stopped a bit, happened to look round and discovered that my friend, stark naked, was dancing about a hundred yards in rear of me, when he had finished he put on his clothes and went home. He is still alive, and dancing

when inclined. Mr. Whales, who has edited
The Mafeking Mail and brought out daily
editions throughout the siege, had an extraordinary escape yesterday. A 94 lb. shell
came into his office and exploded whilst he
was talking to two other men, wrecking the
place, but providentially only slightly scratch-
ing one man. As he emerged from the *debris*
much shaken, his first remark was, " That the
slip would not be issued to-night." This is the
second shell through the office, and though
the setting up operations are carried on in
a bomb proof, he has consistently carried on
his editorial avocations regardless of the
heaviest fire. This practice I am glad to say
he proposes to discontinue in a measure, and
work more or less underground, for, as he
truly says, " The third shell may hit me."
Really this does look as if it were the
beginning of the end, and as if this somewhat
isolated outpost of the Empire were going to
get its communications with civilization
restored. It has been an experience, and
though certainly not a very pleasant one,
I do not think the survivors can but have
profited by it. I rather fancy, however, that

it will take a singularly astute foeman ever to involve any of them in a siege again ; it is, however, Colonel Vyvyan's second experience in South Africa, as he was once before shut up in Etchowe.

March 1st. Yesterday a large party of women and children, who do not belong to this district, were sent away ; the Boers turned them back, and when they were retiring deliberately opened a heavy fire on them, killing and wounding many. This is not the first deliberate outrage on the native women and children, and in addition they have flogged and turned back women trying to escape. Colonel Baden-Powell has addressed several remonstrances to General Snyman on the subject, and pointed out that he cannot expect the native chiefs in the vicinity to restrain their tribesmen, if the Boers persist in murdering their friends and relations, and that he, Colonel Baden-Powell, cannot be answerable for any subsequent occurrences in the way of reprisals on the part of the natives, to which General Snyman has answered as a rule more or less civilly (generally less) that we and the natives may do our worst. To-day

11

is the usual sort of day, heavy sniping at intervals and a fair amount of shelling. Certainly the amount of damage done to Mafeking in life and property has been wholly disproportionate to the amount of shell fire sustained, the reason of course being the soft mud bricks of which the houses are constructed ; and to-day we had two very fine object lessons of the extensive damage these shells would have done among more solidly constructed edifices. Mr. Whitely, the mayor's, house, which is built of stronger materials than any other house in Mafeking, was struck by a shell, and the damage done was far greater than was usually the case. Round the house of Mr. Bell, the magistrate, there is a loose stone wall, the shell struck and exploded at the base of it, the fragments of shell did but little harm, but one boulder about twice the size of a man's body was hurled about twenty-five yards, and two rocks about twice the size of a man's head were projected through the house some twenty-five yards away, while stones of various sizes were hurled great distances and in every direction. So, though thanks to its flimsy construction, Mafeking has escaped better than many a more important town would, it does seem rather like breaking a butterfly to use modern siege guns against a place of this sort. However, it is still a fairly lively butterfly in spite of twelve thousand pounds of metal from one gun alone. We have developed a new trench N.E. of the town to enfilade the enemies' sniping trenches, which, though it does not silence them, seems to annoy them passably.

2nd. Shell fire. Our new gun was tried on the sniping trenches, more for ranging purposes and to learn her extent and powers than anything else. The Boer trenches showed great curiosity as to what she was and why she did it, for her shells burst with a most delightful report and seemed to spread very nicely. A new toy like this is a god-send to us in our present dull condition.

The Boers during the experiment, however, kept themselves and their curiosity underground. The Boer big gun was removed at sunset and the usual crop of surmises, bets as to destination, cause of removal, &c., sprang rapidly into existence, and at any rate gave us something to

11 *

talk about ; it takes very little to interest us here.

3rd. The Boers tried dynamiting our trenches last night, but failed, our advanced parties are within forty yards of each other. At dawn the big gun, which had shifted back to the south-east heights from where she flanks our brickfield advance, commenced heavy fire, sending thirty-six or thirty-eight shells before breakfast, and mortally wounding Sergeant-Major Taylor of the Cape Boys; we also had four or five others wounded more or less severely. They, however, stuck to their ground in shallow trenches which were hardly any protection, and that we suffered no greater loss is a matter of astonishment to everybody.

Our seven-pounders then commenced on their trenches, and the firing was heavy all round the whole morning. The Boers contemplated renewing their entertainment in the afternoon, but our snipers had crept up to within about eight hundred yards of the big gun and commenced picking off the gunners. Trooper Webb, C. P., fortunately shot their Artillery Officer whilst laying the gun, at a fairly early stage in the performance, and this seemed to damp their enthusiasm. They commenced running about like a lot of disturbed ants, messengers were dispatched to the laager, their doctor arrived on horseback, and they then proceeded to hoist three Red Cross flags on the work. They carried a stretcher under a guard towards the laager and met a carriage, but he was apparently too bad to be put in that, and the carriage returned to the laager, when some mounted men rode forth, and, meeting the stretcher, dismounted and followed behind. Altogether they seemed very depressed whilst we were correspondingly the reverse, and in the confusion the big gun forgot to go off, and was removed before dark. With the exception of musketry the rest of the day was quiet. Our saps have now crossed each other.

Sunday. This morning at daybreak the Boers were still working, so we gave them a volley at forty yards and are believed to have shot four. Sniping continued all day, and later on we killed another. From this quarter the Boers, who were evidently very cross, sniped viciously all day. I walked up with Captain Williams, whose turn it is now for duty in the brickfields, and personally I consider it a most undesirable place of residence. The big gun has disappeared. We are all glad to hear that our old friend Cronje is in a tight place; from all accounts he will trouble us no more.

5th. The big gun is back at the old place east of the town; her immediate *entourage* evidently prefer gun practice at a safe range, for we have shot a good many gunners. Their efforts to get the gun off under musketry fire always cause amusement. They rush to the gun, and then disappear, this goes on sometimes quite a long time before the gun gets fired. Sergeant Major Taylor died last night; he was a splendid fellow and a good representative of the Cape Boys, who are a most gallant race of men and good shots. In times of peace he was one of the leading members of the Church in the location. There is heavy firing in the direction of the brickfields, so I must see what is going on.

6th. Yesterday our seven-pounders made very good shooting on the Boer brickfield trenches, and after Mr. Feltham, Protectorate Regiment, had thrown dynamite at them for some time, the Cape Boys went to poke them out of their sap with the bayonet, but the wily Boer was gone ; they had closed their sap. In this fight of " sit down " (as the Zulus say), I for one had worn out much patience and several pairs of trousers, and we seem to be borrowing more and more hints in the way of mortars, hand grenades, &c., from our forefathers. The Boers seemed much annoyed yesterday afternoon, and heavy firing went on last night and is going on this morning. The big gun did not fire yesterday though she was elevated and pointed several times, nor has she fired this morning. There are strong rumours that the Boers intend to trek, and are preparing for it; that the gun we see is a dummy; and that the real one has been withdrawn to defend a position on the frontier. We sincerely hope it is true.

6th. The gun proved herself to be the " old original " by letting us have two or three shots in the evening.

7th. Heavy firing all night in the brick-fields ; only two shells. The Boers have commenced to trek. Trooper McDonald, Cape Police, died. His was an adventurous

career ; he joined the Argyle and Sutherland
Highlanders in '47, served in the Crimea
(French and Sardinian Medal, two clasps),
served in the Indian Mutiny, was kidnapped
when embarking home by Americans, fought
for the North against the South, deserted the
North and fought for the South, afterwards
went to Australia, thence to New Zealand,
and served in the Maori War where he was
taken prisoner. Later he came to South
Africa, served in the Basuto War, Sir Charles
Warren's expedition, Carrington's Horse, the
B. B. P., and transferred to the Cape Police,
in which corps he has died of hardships and
old age, fighting the Boers. He is not the
only Crimean veteran we have here, both the
Navy and Army are represented. Mr. Ellis
joined the Royal Navy in 1854, served in the
Baltic and the Black Sea, came to Africa and
served in the Galika War. Mr. Brasier served
in the Crimea and Mutiny, and there are
others of whose extent of service I am not so
certain. The contrast between them and the
Cadet Corps, who are utilised for orderly
work, &c., is remarkable, and if the Boers
have their greybeards and boys fighting, why

so have we. It seems very curious at first, but one soon gets used to it, as indeed one does to the underground residences, all business, as far as possible, being carried on in dug-outs ; dining-rooms, offices, stores, barracks, even the bank where Mr. Urry, who with Captain Greener runs our paper coinage, sits in charge of a vast amount of paper, but very little hard cash, for the Kaffirs have buried all specie obtainable, are below ground. In our dug-out we have some siege mice, born since its construction, of a friendly and confiding disposition, who come and feed on the table, and play about and have a good time generally; other animals are therefore not admitted.

8th. Good news arrived of Cronje's defeat and surrender, and the wiping out of Majuba Day. Soldiers were proud, the population at large delighted, but most of all the South African Englishman. For the last twenty years he has been taunted by the Dutch with Majuba ; he can now hold up his head again, and nothing could conduce more to a permanent pacification of South Africa than the wiping out of the day. Henning Pretorius, one of the leading Transvaal burghers, when he heard of Majuba, said, "Now it is finished. They will never stop till they have wiped us out." This he maintained till his death, which occurred recently, and he always urged that the Boers should make friends with us and become one nation. Usual heavy firing at night, only one shell.

9th. Heavy firing all night, commencing early with heavy volleys on the north and north-west fronts. I rode round the western outposts ; it is a very pleasant ride and the Boers were pretty quiet, at least as concerned me, for they took no notice at all.

10th. Heavy firing this morning in the brickfields, the gun is elevated and pointed on the town, in which position she has remained for the past two or three days with very occasional shells. The Boers are daily treking by degrees. I propose to go down to the brickfields this morning as that is about the liveliest spot in Mafeking, though I fancy very little of it will go a long way.

Trooper Webb of the Cape Police was shot through the head in the brickfield trenches last night; a fine specimen of a splendid corps. He was shot through the ankle in a sortie at the commencement of the siege, and when able to hobble he came out for duty as look-out man and orderly at headquarters; yesterday, as he was not so lame, at his earnest request he was allowed to go on duty in the advanced trenches, and during his first tour of sentry-go, was mortally wounded by a chance bullet in the dark. He is greatly regretted by the townspeople and all ranks, and Her Majesty loses a fine soldier, a firstclass policeman, and a good all-round man.

I went down to the brickfields this morning and met Captain Fitzclarence and Captain Williams; things were pretty quiet down there in the morning, though they livened up again shortly afterwards. I went round the trenches with them. One's mode of progression is distinctly uncomfortable, bent double, with a certain amount of water in the trenches, which are shallow as yet between the various works, but being deepened daily. The various works and trenches all have their names, Regent's Circus, Oxford Street, &c., whilst our most advanced work is called the New Cut, and the Boers' trench forty yards away Houndsditch. The sound of the

Mauser at this short range has a very different effect to its sound at the longer ranges, and the crack of the bullets when they strike is like the explosion of a young shell. The Boers at these ranges are very quick and good shots; they shoot at your hat if visible, or at the sound of your voice, and as the loopholes have to be kept closed, the only way of looking out is by means of a pair of Zeiss glasses which project over the edge of the parapet while one's head is in safety some inches below, even so they put a bullet through one of the lenses this morning (which, as they were mine, did not please me) and through the hat of the look-out man, but with them you can see right into the Boer loopholes with comparative safety, though bullets frequently, owing to the tremendous penetration of the Mauser, come clean through the upper part of the parapet, and the sand bags on the top are cut to ribbons. The advance post is occupied by the Cape Boys, who under Lieutenants Feltham and Currie (who has recently been promoted) take it day and day about; one was shot this morning. This post which we now occupy was sapped up to and occupied from the other side by the Boers, but was retaken by the Cape Boys under Currie, with Captain Fitzclarence and some of the white garrison; they had to emerge in single file from a narrow opening which was commanded by the Boer loop-holes, and run round the edge of the excavation of the brickfield up to the loop-holes occupied by the Boers, a distance of some twenty yards; the latter fled on their approach. We have now occupied it from our side and strengthened the work. The trenches approaching the advance works are exposed to fire from the front and right flanks, but are being strengthened daily. On our return from the advance work we made our way to the river bed where Currie's post is established, and it was there that poor Webb was killed. The garrison of the trenches are now fairly housed and comparatively safe, though, of course, casualties occur daily; still, if the Boers try a sortie they will meet a very warm reception.

Sunday. Last night heavy firing as usual, but to-day, contrary to our late custom, peace has reigned in the brickfields, and both sides sat on their parapets and asked after various friends on the other side. The Boers have lately, as the natives express it, become much more tame, and have allowed Kaffir women to gather wood, pumpkins, and Kaffir corn without molestation. Our Sunday was absolutely peaceful and quiet, and as we are not able now to indulge in mounted sports, &c., owing to the condition of the horses, we have fallen back on cricket as our Sunday relaxation.

12th. The natives went out last night, and McKenzie's boys got into Jackal Tree which they found empty. The Baralongs attacked Fort Snyman from the rear and had a lively engagement with the hundred odd Boers who garrisoned it, and after finishing their ammunition, withdrew with a loss of one killed and two wounded. We know of one Boer dead for certain, for Trooper Webb of the C. P. blew his head off at the entrance to the work, and we fancy that at the short range our volleys must have accounted for several more. General Snyman has returned and notified his arrival by an unusually heavy dose of shell fire. I rode round the western outposts this morning with Captain Wilson ; the natives seemed quite pleased with themselves, more

particularly as they had secured some thirty
head of fat cattle in a raid two days ago. We
then inspected the soup kitchens which he is
managing, and which are a great improvement
on those first started ; the food provided is
very popular with the natives, who come in
their hundreds for it.

13th. Our runners brought us in good
news of the relief of Ladysmith and the heavy
Boer losses. Everybody is consequently
jubilant, and our only regret is that we can't
drive these Boers over the frontier and clear
British territory; however, Colonel Plumer
is at Lobatsi, and as there cannot be any
considerable body of Boers between this and
Kimberley, we ought soon to have the line
open both ways. They began shelling early
and kept on with their home-made shrapnel
all day, killing two and wounding several.
One shell burst in a pigeon-house and killed
sixteen valuable carrier pigeons ; the shot is
somewhat large for pigeon shooting, but
apparently effective. The base of another
shell went through the head-quarter office,
making a hideous mess, but hurting no one ; in
fact, they were shooting offices all round, and

the ordinarily neatly-kept official papers were
in two or three cases much upset and covered
with the *debris* of their various abodes.   This
new shrapnel is essentially a man-killing shell,
for which reason I suppose the Boers have
paid particular attention to the earthworks,
per contra if they want to snipe cattle or slay
men they generally employ common shell.
Last night a cattle raiding party came in with
some horses, saddles, rifles and bandoliers
belonging to some deceased Boers.   The
Boers had tracked this party of Baralongs,
who, seeing them following on their spoor,
had doubled back on their own trail and
ambushed them at short range. They accounted
for six or seven, and relieved their dead of
their arms, &c., as far as they could, before the
Boers recovered from their surprise, and drove
them off with a loss to the raiders of one
killed and two wounded, the latter of whom
they brought in.   This success has naturally
much pleased the natives, and encouraged them
greatly for future raids, which is most useful, as
the results feed us and harass the Boers.   The
advanced trenches also got a couple by moonlight as they were creeping up to our trench.

14th. Shelling has begun again this morning, quite up to its best form. The Boers in Snyman's absence take things much more easily, and if we could only kill him here and Kruger in the south, as well as old Cronje, it would save a vast amount of trouble, for it takes these leaders all their time to keep their followers up to the scratch. They had a sort of " indaba " this morning. I only trust it was bad news for them, they get their news about a fortnight before we do.

15th. Fairly quiet day, pretty heavy shelling.

16th. Very little shelling. The Cape Boys in the advance trenches were playing a concertina, and so chaffed the Boers, saying they were dancing, and asking them to send some ladies, &c., that one of them, either attracted by the music or bursting with repartee, popped up his head, and was incontinently shot by a wily Cape Boy, to the intense delight of the others. They have a distinct sense of humour, though possibly a somewhat grim one. The advance trenches are now deepened and strengthened, and are as safe as it is possible for them to be to walk

12

about in; from the advance trenches the
Boers and ourselves throw bombs, and
they are also using explosive bullets ; their
bombs are made like old hand-grenades, the
bombs of both sides being charged with
dynamite. They throw theirs by hand,
but ours, though of a cruder form (being
mainly jam tins) are propelled in a much
more scientific manner. Sergeant Page, of
the Protectorate Regiment, has rigged up
a bamboo as a fishing-rod, and casts his bomb
with great precision the short distance to the
Boer trenches.

17th. Pretty quiet day. Last night
McKenzie's boys raided Jackal Tree fort,
killed one Boer and a Kaffir, and secured
three horses and rifles. The dug-outs are
all so close to various residences that it was
amusing to see one card party, disturbed by
the ringing of the bell, dive from the mess to
the dug-out, and actually be back picking up
their cards before the shell which had passed
high in the air, had exploded. Vices in time of
peace become virtues in war time ; the most
expert Baralong cattle thief, who under
other circumstances would assuredly be in

durance vile, is now indeed a *persona grata*
and leader of men, and whilst enjoying
himself at the top of his bent is making the
most of his fleeting opportunity.

18th, Sunday. I went down to the brickfields to the advanced trenches; down there
both parties had agreed not to shoot, and
exchanged tobacco for peach brandy, &c.,
asking after their various friends and relations.
I got three snap shots at the Boers in the
advance trench, and we studied each other
with great curiosity, our clean shirts, collars,
and Sunday clothes apparently astonishing
them as much as their remarkable grime
surprised us. On the way back there is
a pleasant meadow, in which we lay and
smoked and tried to pretend it was England,
though that was somewhat a failure. Whilst
down there I met an old warrior who had
drifted a long way from his last fight.
A native of Bagdad, he was in Sarif (?) Pasha's
command at Plevna, which he said was a very
different siege to this ; he says they fought
only occasionally there, and then killed
thousands of men, but rested in between,
whilst here we were continually shooting. If

we killed thousands here the siege would soon
come to an end. The old man is very fit and
seems to enjoy his fighting still. Runners
came in from the south this morning who had
seen the relief of Kimberley, which impressed
them very much. They said that the man who
wrote the Bible must have been referring to
the English army, when he spoke of the
Tribes of Israel and the thousands which
composed them, and that the aforesaid army
was big enough to eat up all the Kaffirs; they
reported, also, that the searchlights of the force
advancing up the line had been seen as far as
Taungs, and that the Boers were concentrat-
ing, but are pretty thick between here and the
advancing force. As regards this place the
boot will soon be on the other leg, as the
Boers are now afraid to move about except in
large bodies, and we hope that our communication will soon be thoroughly restored. The
runners from Setlagoli reported that the
raiding party I spoke of on the 13th, had
killed and wounded some twenty Boers,
including the man who had shot one of our
Baralongs in cold blood the day before.
There was a smoking concert to-night to

celebrate St. Patrick's Day, largely attended
by Irishmen and others; the proceedings were
harmonious throughout.

19th. A fair amount of shelling. A party
of Boers and three guns have returned from
the north, where native rumour says they
have had a repulse, and in which direction
musketry fire was faintly heard yesterday
morning.

20th. We got runners in from the north ;
the Boers seem in a bad way all round.

21st. More runners in. To-day we were
unlucky, and we had a few casualties.

22nd. More runners. Plumer's column
twenty-four miles away.

23rd. We shelled the brickfield trench,
but did not succeed in drawing fire from the
big gun, which has been almost silent for the
last few days. In the garrison there are
soldiers from all parts of the world, one
German veteran who served all through the
Franco-German War in the 84th Regiment,
Trooper Block by name, was through the
Orleans campaign, and has since served in
all the South African wars ; there are men
who served in the Chilian war, the Carlist,

and in fact practically every known war for the last fifty years.

24th. Last night the Boers evacuated their brickfield trenches, which we occupied with much cheering ; they left several cases of dynamite behind connected with a wire, with which they proposed to blow up our men ; the wire was, however, promptly disconnected. In Dutch newspapers discovered in the trenches was found the account of the fall of Bloemfontein, which was confirmed by runners from Plumer this morning. The Boers have now withdrawn to a respectful distance all round the town, which is, however, still invested, but the big gun so far is quiet. This must be the beginning of the end, and we have nearly completed our six months' siege. I fully expect the big gun to be removed in a day or two ; last night was the first time she has failed to reply to our artillery fire.

We have started a post-office here, with stamps, &c., and also a very tastefully designed £1 note. I must finish off my entries as a go of fever makes it difficult, almost impossible, to write at all.

24th. Last night Sub-Inspector Murray and Trooper Melahue, Cape Police, went out, and having reconnoitred the rear of the enemy's trench, came to the conclusion that it was unoccupied. Inspector Browne, of the Cape Police, and the Cape Boys under Lieutenants Feltham and Currie, proceeded to occupy it. The Boers had left a mine of 250 lbs. of nitro-glycerine behind. Sergeant Page, Protectorate Regiment, discovered and disconnected the wire. The men cheered themselves hoarse, and rightly too, for this is the most decisive success we have scored since the commencement of the campaign, as the town is now for the first time free from musketry fire, and our guns are again within striking distance of the Boer artillery.

25th, Sunday. The Siege Exhibition took place to-day. A most creditable exhibition from the ingenuity shown, and also considering its peculiar surroundings. We shall hope to forward some of our exhibits home. I went out and inspected the Boer trench. If it is "an ill bird that fouls its own nest," a Boer is indeed ill. They are occupying a trench about seven hundred yards away, from which they shoot with a certain amount of precision, but with no result, upon their late happy home. Personally, I particularly wished to inspect the brick kilns, at which I had discharged some hundred rounds of ammunition. It is very interesting, but still somewhat annoying to find that it is practically bullet proof ; however, on the other hand, the particular place of resort from which I had fired the said ammunition was also fairly safe, so perhaps I had no reason to grumble, and at any rate I had frequently silenced them.

26th, Monday. Exceptionally quiet to-day. Late at night I was in Mr. Weil's dug-out when he received the news of the English troops' arrival at Vryburg. Mafeking accordingly jubilant.*

27th, Tuesday. The Boers commenced early and continued a heavy shell fire all day, pouring more shells into the town than they had any two days of the siege. It was very curious, but the news received the night before caused the population to show more absolute disregard for the shell fire than they

---

* This eventually turned out to be untrue.

had done on many days when the bombardment was comparatively light. The Premier's message to the two Presidents was published this evening, and now even the most pessimistic admit it is possible that there may be a satisfactory solution of the war. We hope we may be able to slightly assist in a less passive manner than heretofore.

28th, Wednesday. After our treat of yesterday, absolute quiet reigns to-day. Really there is no understanding the Boers. Our locally manufactured field-piece burst last night, but the shell managed to reach the Boer laager. What they contemplate and what is their plan of campaign leaves everybody wondering. No ulterior object can be obtained by their desultory mode of conducting operations. Occasional casualties, which is apparently their only object, is the sole result arrived at, and these casualties are, we think, more heavy on their side than ours.

29th, Thursday. A quiet day. The Boers gradually evacuating their eastern trenches.

30th, Friday. The guns are fairly quiet. We are gradually occupying the evacuated trenches.

31st, Saturday. In the morning a quiet day. In the afternoon a body of four hundred or five hundred Boers and three guns hastily left their eastern laager in a northerly direction. I took up a position in the convent, and from there could see considerable confusion and excitement amongst the Boers galloping backwards and forwards in the direction of Signal Hill. The sound of guns too was distinctly audible to the north, some six or seven miles away. The garrison livened up. The guns under Major Panzera and Lieutenant Daniells commenced playing from every face. A mounted squadron under Major Godley demonstrated towards Game Tree fort on the north. For an hour or so things were lively, but quieted down.

Our old " Lord Nelson " reached the laager, and the big gun was annoyed by the Hotchkiss. It is a curious fact that all the pieces of ordnance with which we are " blessed " are obsolete naval guns. Rumours as usual flying around and we really had something to give scope for conjecture.

April 1st, Sunday. The siege as affecting me pecuniarily is becoming expensive. I lose bets at the end of each month as it interminably prolongs.

A quiet day and a flag of truce from the Boers asking us to fetch our dead who were killed in the northern fight the day before. Accordingly wagons under Lieutenant the Honourable Hanbury Tracy and Lieutenant Singleton went north, where they met the Boers, who assisted them to find and recover the bodies. Three men were brought in belonging to Colonel Plumer's column, and Captain McLaren, Lieutenant Crewe, and Troopers Murray and Robinson were reported wounded. It would seem to have been a sharp skirmish between a strong patrol of Colonel Plumer's and a considerably more numerous body of Boers, but as far as we can ascertain Colonel Plumer's main column was not engaged.

Our demonstration against Game Tree resulted in our killing two Boers, and even by their own accounts, numerically our losses were evenly balanced. Fourteen dead horses were seen on the field.

2nd, Monday. Flags of truce from the enemy reporting the death of Captain McLaren.

Regret and sympathy barely express my own
feelings, and how many of us are there scattered about the world, who when they see the
next polo tournament, will think again of the
best of players, the nicest of fellows, whom
Hurlingham and the scenes of his many
triumphs will see no more.

There seems a chance of another fight this
afternoon. The Boers are very restless and
galloping about in all directions. I do not
suppose they mean to attack us, and, as far
as I can make out, are nervous and seem to
expect pressure from the east.

Some men were interviewed yesterday who
had returned from Natal. They reported the
death of Joubert and were far less confident
than they have shown themselves heretofore.

3rd, Tuesday. I am heartily glad to say
that Captain McLaren is not dead, although
severely wounded and a prisoner in the Boers'
hands.

A despatch was received from Colonel
Plumer this morning stating that he had had
an engagement north of the town and that
his losses were Captain Crewe (who was
buried here this morning), Lieutenant

Milligan, killed ; Colonel Plumer, Major
Weston Jarvis, and Captain Rolt, slightly
wounded ; non-commissioned Officers and
men killed, seven ; wounded, twenty-six ;
missing, eleven. Three missing are known
to be dead and the others are wounded in the
Boers' hands. Captain McLaren has written
from the Boer camp, where he is, we are
all glad to hear, going on well and being very
well treated by the Boers.

Yesterday afternoon we had a successful
brush with the enemy to north-west, no
casualties on our side. Their ambulances
were seen very busy. To-day everything is
so far quiet.

4th. Early this morning Lieutenant F.
Smitheman, Rhodesian Regiment, Colonel
Plumer's intelligence officer, arrived through
the Boer lines. I met him as he was going to
change. He said, " How do you do ?
I am —— glad to be in." I said, " How are
you ? I am very glad to see you, but
I should be —— glad to be out." However,
there is no satisfying everybody. The
country was infested by Boers and he had
walked twenty-two miles that night accom-

panied by two natives. He is as a scout *facile princeps*, and thus eluded the hostile cordon successfully, though he had one anxious moment when he fell into the trench connecting Fort Ayr and the refugee laager, heard native voices, and was for some time under the impression it was the Boer trench. He was second in command of Colonel Plumer's scouts in 1896, and afterwards disappeared into Central Africa for two years, going from Chinde to Blantyre, to Lake Nyassa, then by Lake Bangueolo to the source of the Congo, thence due south through the Mashakalumbwe country to Victoria Falls, and through which country he was the first white man to pass, and from the falls to Bulawayo, where he arrived in December, 1898. Though his journeys then may have been long, arduous, and dangerous, they can scarcely have been more exciting than the short twenty-two miles he walked last night.

A quiet day. Flags of truce pass daily informing us of the condition of the wounded.

5th, Thursday. This morning Smitheman went to the brickfields with the Colonel and was shot at a bit. We all told him that we were afraid we shouldn't be able to find him any entertainment as the Boers are very quiet just now, and he said we needn't trouble. However, as the morning wore on the enemy's sixteen-pounder commenced bombarding us from Game Tree and Jackal Tree and kept on the whole morning, apparently directed by a deserter, Private Hay, Protectorate Regiment, who selected his late fort and the headquarters of the Protectorate Regiment, as his main target. I shouldn't care to be Private Hay after the war as there is £50 on his head, dead or alive, and the Boers are hard up. The afternoon was pretty quiet, and the Boers have now retired all round to extreme musketry range of all the town. They livened up in the evening though, and fired a good deal, landing many bullets in the square.

6th, Friday. The morning began very quietly, and we were afraid that Smitheman would not get his introduction to "Creaky." However, in the afternoon she began, and he had a full opportunity of learning the meaning of the various sounds of the bell,

13

the joys of the rush to the "dug-out," and the philosophy with which you can see your friends in the distance shelled, when she diverted a certain portion of her fire on Cannon Kopje.

Major Goold-Adams had just shifted into a new office after his former one had been destroyed, and somewhat prematurely, for "Creaky" promptly blew it up with the first shell ; fortunately it was empty at the time. They gave us a good doing and stopped for the night.

7th, Saturday. We were awakened by the big gun, which kept on all day. Smitheman was again lucky. He went up to lunch at the kopje, and then they began shelling that, so he had had most of the pleasures of Mafeking compressed into three days. They pall, however, after six months. He seemed to think we were having a harder time than he anticipated, and it is very interesting to have an outside opinion, because we are so thoroughly used to it that we do not know whether it is a bad time or not, being only convinced of two things—that the place can't fall, and that we will not get hit by a big

shell if we can help it.   Smitheman returned
to Plumer to-night.

8th, Sunday.   A quiet day.   A body of
women, who, at Smitheman's instigation, was
endeavouring to escape towards Kanya, where
food is ready for them, was turned back by
the Boers.   To the south a similar body was
also stopped, and by direction of the Boer in
charge each one was stripped, shambokked,
and driven back naked to Mafeking.   Yesterday there was a desperate fight between a
party of our Fingoes engaged in cattle raiding
and the Boers; the former were cut off and
surrounded in a " pan," where they took what
cover they could and defended their lives to
the last.   Out of a party of some thirty odd,
ten or eleven got away when they repulsed
the first attack of the Boers.   The Boers
returned, however, with one hundred more
men, and killed all but one man.   They
had two Maxims and a one-pound Maxim-
Nordenfelt.   The fight lasted twenty-five hours,
and by the account of the wounded survivor,
corroborated by the women who returned
to-day, the Boers must have suffered severe
loss.   The survivor escaped by hiding in the

13 *

reeds, and is now in hospital with a wound in his stomach. The natives were vastly out-numbered, and made a stubborn resistance with their obsolete arms against all the Boers could bring against them. Unfortunate it is that so few of many brave men escaped.

Snyman is becoming remarkably civil in his intercourse, and had sent in a letter saying he was astonished that natives had been employed cattle raiding, as they were such barbarians. They were right gallant barbarians, anyhow. Smitheman has a wonderful insight into native character, and a marvellous grasp of the Baralong. It is curious to note how the Eng-lishman associated with the natives identifies himself with his tribe and ·becomes a Zulu, Baralong, Fingoe or Basuto with a firm belief that all other natives except his own particular tribe are no good at all and that their methods of fighting are useless. Having heard the point discussed by many of my friends and having witnessed their implicit confidence in their own particular tribe and distrust of the others, one can understand that the foreigner may see some-thing to laugh at in an Englishman's absolute and justified confidence in the English. They call it insularity in Europe. I wonder what they would call its offspring here.

9th, Monday. Runners from the north arrived with the intelligence that Smitheman had passed them well clear of the Boer line, so we hope he is safe. The big gun has been shelling all the morning, and some of her smaller brethren have taken it up this afternoon. Many conflicting rumours, but a force of many men and guns went south on Friday night. We hope this portends the approach of our expected relief. It would be hard lines indeed, after all this dull work, not to finish the campaign in the Transvaal. The natives say the Boers are going to give us another severe doing to-morrow. The flags of truce exchange much chaff. The Boers say, "Why don't you come out and fight in the open?" and the answer is, "Come and drive us out." The other day the Boers said to our orderly that it was very brutal sending men who had never been to sea to St. Helena, besides what would they do there? Whether he expected us to find picnic parties for them or not I do not know. I wish I were at

St. Helena, one would have a chance of getting
somewhere else from there.   The orderly said
there was plenty to do, but the Boer objected
there were no horses for them to ride, and when
the orderly said, " Let them ride the turtles,"
he was very wroth.   Again, yesterday, the
Boer volunteered that they, the Dutch, were
knocking us about in the Free State.   The
orderly said, " The Free State, where is the
Free State ? " and the Boer said, " North of
the Orange River."   On the orderly's answering, " Ah ! You mean New England," the
Boer seemed hurt, but they are pretty
civil all the same and both sides continually ask after their various friends and
get answers.

10th, Tuesday.   A fairly quiet day.   The
high velocity guns shelled our outlying posts
on the western border, with occasional shots
at the camp, while the big gun and the smaller
ones shelled the town.   Natives from the
south report that the country is at present
unsafe for despatch riders as, though there is
no commando, there are a considerable number
of Boers roaming about the country between
here and Vryburg seeking whom and what

PEACEFUL TALK BETWEEN BOERS AND BRITISH.

By permission of " The Daily Graphic."

they may devour and under no immediate
control.*

11th, Wednesday. We were awakened this
morning by the big gun and had a very heavy
day's shelling. I went out for a ride and up
to Fort Ayr. They were shelling from every
side in all directions and kept it up till nearly
noon. Mr. Greenfield is at present doing his
month's detachment duty at Fort Ayr. It is
not an enlivening spot, being built underground, and as you are continually sniped it
is impossible to emerge therefrom except at
night or by means of a long rear trench leading to the refugees' laager. It is garrisoned
by thirty men, a Maxim and a seven-pounder.
On the western front the Boers made an
attack on two of our outlying posts. They
advanced to within four hundred and fifty
yards, but after losing some ten or a dozen
men they retired. During the day they
planted some thirty shells into the women's
laager. To all their heavy bombardment we
answered not a shot, but in the evening when
they were dismantling the big gun the Hotch-

---

* Later they themselves were devoured.

kiss opened on her with good effect, apparently wounding or killing several of the crowd round her. She immediately opened fire on the town and struck the Dutch Church with great violence. After she had ceased firing the Hotchkiss opened again and failed to get a further reply. Score :—Hotchkiss four, big gun three.

12th, Thursday. This morning the big gun has disappeared and is supposed to be in McMullin's laager. She has not fired, and with the exception of the five-pounder we have had a quiet day.

Several wagons with escorts have trekked from the laager and they are apparently busily engaged in packing up others.

A pigeon left Colonel Plumer yesterday at noon arriving here in forty minutes, and runners in this morning brought Her Majesty's message to Colonel Baden-Powell and news of Lieutenant Smitheman's safe arrival at Colonel Plumer's camp.

Captain McLaren is, I am glad to say, better, and in the hands of a skilful German surgeon who thinks he will do all right.

The rains have begun again which is

fortunate for us. Had it not been for the exceptionally rainy season I do not know what the cattle would have done or how we could have held out.

13th, Friday. A quiet day. We were only shelled to-day with the five-pounder and the one-pound Maxim and so we are quite quiet. Colonel Baden-Powell has had an erection built on the top of the headquarter house from whence he looks out and can control the Mafeking defences like the captain of a ship, shouting his instructions down a speaking tube to the headquarter bomb proof, which are thence telephoned on to the parties whom it may concern, so that he can personally turn on the tap of any portion of the defences he may think fit.

14th, Saturday. This morning there was quite a lively amount of shelling. One shell burst in Fort Ayr and killed two of its garrison. Personally I started for a ride, but finding it rather livelier than I cared for made it a pretty short one. One must get exercise, but there is no particular object in getting shot unnecessarily. Last night Colonel Plumer's column endeavoured to send us in some hundred head of cattle which we want. It was a moonlight night and the Boers must have been informed of their advent for they waylaid them very effectually, killing and wounding many, as well as their native drivers, and capturing the rest. This is a bore, but, however, we can get on without them and we shall get them back shortly. In consequence of this diversion they were firing pretty well all night. Easter Day to-morrow. We can do very well without the Easter eggs the Boers send us, and as our hens have ceased to lay we shall get none of our own. Our hot cross buns were represented by a cross being stamped on our scanty bread ration. I rather hope that this is the last feast of any sort that the garrison of Mafeking will celebrate under siege conditions.

Colonel Vyvyan was very lucky in securing a beautiful specimen of a sixteen-pounder, Vicker's Maxim, which passed over his head and did not explode. In the scurry for the shell he secured it, as he was mounted. They are using a new sort of one-pound Maxim and not being quite able to reach the women's laager with it they planted six shells in the

By permission of "The Daily Graphic."

A SHELL BURSTING IN THE NATIVE QUARTER.

hospital. Yesterday one of Colonel Plumer's wounded died while undergoing an operation in the Boer camp and they sent his body in last night.

I cannot understand the Boer, and have given it up as a bad job. He appears to have no laws and few instincts, and to be totally irresponsible. Sometimes he behaves exceedingly well, and at other times remarkably ill, and you can never calculate what his conduct will be under any given circumstances. General Snyman is sanctimonious and a hypocrite, and seems to look upon truth as an unnecessary portion of his field outfit. Commandant Botha is a good sportsman, and well liked on their side of the border, and is a kindly dispositioned man. Snyman is a strict disciplinarian as Boers go, whilst Botha seems an easier going man. If Snyman has been away, on his return the more or less quiet existence we have led, thanks to Botha, is immediately disturbed, and heavy shell fire commences. Snyman is not popular in Mafeking, the inhabitants of which look upon him as a combination of liar, fanatic and woman killer, and, generally speaking, an infernal nuisance. The Dutch say he is very venturesome; he will, I believe, venture a lot to obtain cattle, but apparently less to obtain Mafeking. The Boers at the outset could have captured Mafeking for about half the lives they have expended in their various futile attacks. They can never capture it now, and the one ardent desire of the garrison is that they may only endeavour to do so.

15th, Sunday, Easter-day. A quiet day and the big gun still undiscoverable. The various churches were well attended at all the services. In the afternoon we had sports, organized by Captain Cowan and the officers of the Bechuanaland Rifles. They were a great success, and the costume race, won by Mr. Daniel, B. S. A. P., dressed as a hospital nurse, Mr. Dunlop Smith, A. V. D., as the "Geisha" second, Captain Scholefield, B. S. A. P., as a bride third, was a great success, and one of the most amusing contests we have had here.

Yesterday it was indeed bad luck for the poor fellows of Fort Ayr garrison who had remained under cover during shell fire and thought it was all over, for when Troopers Molloy and Hassell came out to get their coffee the last high velocity sixteen-pound shell struck the sand bags overhead, killing Molloy dead and mortally wounding Hassell, breaking both his legs. Mr. Greenfield tells me the way he bore his sufferings was literally heroical, complaining not at all, and only asking for a cigarette.

I have not previously alluded to the "sowen" porridge, which is now a part of the rations, and has for a long time done much to solve the question of the food supply of Mafeking. It was first made by Private Sims out of the husks of oats for the consumption of himself and sundry of his comrades, but on this fact being ascertained by the indefatigable Captain Ryan, Sims was put on to make it on a larger scale for the natives. The European portion of the garrison and inhabitants gladly bought it, and it is now, as I said before, an acceptable portion of the daily rations. The natives, too, have had great windfalls lately in the matter of locusts, which are really not bad eating, and at any rate much appreciated by them. The feeding of the natives, indeed, at all times a difficult question, is, I may say, practically solved, except in the case of the Shangans. These unfortunate devils, who are equally repulsive, morally and physically, as far as I have seen, are detested by the other natives, and consequently it is very hard to look after them properly. The Basutos, Zulus, &c., come to be fed naturally, whereas the Shangan is like a wild beast, and only seems to crawl away and die. So much is this so that on Mr. Vere Stent's ordering his Basuto servant to make some soup for a starving Shangan he had picked up, the Basuto indignantly protested that " the Shangans were bad men and killed missionaries," however, the man in question was rescued in time and is still living. They form luckily an insignificant proportion of the native community.

After the siege is over and the Queen has got her own again it is to be hoped that the unswerving loyalty of the Baralongs will not be over-looked. You hear on all sides that the Baralongs are not a fighting race, and the Zulus and any other race you may mention would wipe them out. Incidentally the Zulus

tried to in their big trek north, and the wily
Baralong, fighting his usual fight, had considerably the best of it.

In more modern times he successfully with-
stood the Boers, not, however, an attack on
the present scale. After the first day's shelling the mouthpiece of the Baralong tribe,
Silas Molemo, came up to Mr. Bell, Resident
Magistrate, and said to him, "Never mind
this we will stick to you and see it through,"
which they certainly have done. They
are not a tribe who would make a dashing
attack or to use the expression "be bossed
up" to do things they don't particularly want
to, but given a defensive position they
will hang on to it for all they are worth as
they have proved many times during the war
in their defence of their stadt. They have had
their cattle raided, their out-lying homesteads
destroyed, their crops for this year are *nil*, and
all through a time when the outlook to a native
mind must have seemed most black they have
unswervingly and uncomplainingly stuck to
us and never hesitated to do anything they
were called upon to do.

I cannot do better than give an account of
14 *

the unsuccessful attempt to bring in cattle
from Colonel Plumer. Mathakong, the leader
of the party, had forty men under his command.
He and the Baralongs have so far been very
successful in getting in cattle; by profession
a cattle thief, but only on a large scale,
there is nothing mean about Mathakong.
Colonel Plumer selected some hundred head
of cattle in good condition and it was these
that the party endeavoured to bring in.
When they were some distance out it was
reported to Mathakong that the Boers
knew that they were coming and were going
to try to intercept them. However, as he had
been given to understand that it was desirable
to get the cattle in he determined to make
the attempt, as at any rate they might get
some in, and if he stayed where he was the
Boers would probably surround him. The
Boers got on both flanks of the cattle, assisted
by the Rapulanas (the Rietfontein rebel
natives), and heavy firing began. The Baralongs pushed forward with cattle falling all
round them and behind the bodies of the
cattle kept up a running fight until all their
ammunition was gone. They stuck to them

till only fifteen head were left, and then when they left, the Boers came up cheering loudly. There were two wounded men amongst the cattle and the Boers according to their custom came up and interrogated them and then shot one and cut the other's throat. The Baralongs then came into Mafeking dragging old Matha-kong with them as they could not otherwise persuade him to leave the live cattle. He was much upset by the loss of the cattle, but the fight did not worry him at all, and he said that had the cattle not been in such good condition he would have rushed them along faster and got most of them in. This, how-ever, is only one of the many cases in which the Baralongs have done, or have endeavoured to do good service. They lost four killed and seven wounded and account for their small loss by the protection afforded them by the herd amongst which they fought their running fight.

16th, Monday. Fairly quiet day. The Boers shelled the western outpost and brickfields. I went down to the brickfields to see Captain Brown, Cape Police, who is in charge and was in charge when he occupied

the Boer advanced trench. Since then he
has been wounded, but is now back at duty
again. He told me that the idea of the Boers
was apparently that we should not enter the
trench until the morning after they had
vacated it, but our doing so the night before
and cutting the wire had frustrated their
aimable intention of blowing up our men
and presumably rushing the brickfields in
the confusion. The other day, a Cape
policeman met a Transvaal policeman with
a white flag (between these forces in
times of peace a very good feeling prevails)
and chaffed him, saying, "Why don't you blow
your mine up." "Ah!" said the latter, "you
were too slim for us there." Houndsditch,
the old Boer trench, has now been converted
into a strong fortification for ourselves, and
the brickfields generally are a far more
desirable place for residence, the several Boer
trenches now being nine hundred to one
thousand two hundred yards away. They
have some very good marksmen in their
trenches however, and make things very warm
for our advanced trenches. A Cape Boy
exposed himself for a moment two or three

days ago and was picked off through the head
by a Martini at once, and in the very few
open spaces which of course they have got
accurately ranged they shoot remarkably
close. The brickfields are now garrisoned by
the Cape Police and Cape Boys under Captain
Brown and Lieutenants Murray and Currie.

The big gun is still conspicuous by its
absence, and it is reported to have gone to
Pretoria. If that be so it is the greatest
sign so far that the Boers feel hopeless about
taking the town and the point may be fairly
scored off against any point they may have
scored against us yet.

There was a wedding this morning between
a private of the Bechuanaland Rifles and
a Dutch girl, he cannot talk Dutch nor she
English. Let us hope that it is a good omen
of the future settlement of South Africa with
the British as " Boss."

This morning, too, three ambulances were
seen coming in from the North, and an
ambulance and five waggons went in that
direction, so Plumer may have had a successful
" scrap," at any rate, we all hope so.

These high velocity guns seem beautiful

weapons, I must confess that in common with the rest of the garrison I should dearly like to see them tried on the Boer. It is all very well to be an expert in artillery, but ours is not the most agreeable way of gaining the experience.

17th, Tuesday. The question of firewood and indeed all fuel has of late been a somewhat serious one to Mafeking, and as the cold season is coming on or rather is beginning, increases in importance daily, consequently Mafeking has had to sacrifice its scanty supply of trees. Probably the residents in their vicinity wish, if they had to be cut down, it had been done at the commencement of the siege, for it seems as if the Boer artillery when having no mark in particular but the town in general had mainly aimed at the trees, at any rate, when they were merely idly shelling the majority of shells fell in their neighbourhood. It will, I fear, put the general appearance of the town back for some years.

With the exception of perfunctory shelling in the brickfields, we have had a quiet day and the big gun is still absent. Indeed, now so far have our outlying trenches been pushed

that except from the big gun and quick-firers,
we experience but little annoyance in the town
itself. During the last week our runners have
been most successfully stopped, but before this
we have been fortunate enough to get London
papers three months old, and the Court House
has been turned into a reading-room, where
the papers are daily eagerly devoured by all
conditions of men and women too. Everybody
at home seems very pleased with Mafeking,
and we here feel really proud of the way our
fellows are fighting in the South and the way
everybody is turning up to fight. It should
be a fine object-lesson to the Continentals.
In many ways they must have had a more
amusing time than we have had and fighting on
a much larger scale, for this sort of fighting
after the first two months is about the dullest
sort of entertainment you can well imagine:
they so hopelessly overwhelm us in artillery
that we cannot get out to have a go at them.
Indeed, any sortie must resolve itself into storming one of their forts which we are not strong
enough to do, and so the forts on either side
face each other, fire at each other, but otherwise
leave each other severely alone; and outside

their zone of fire their artillery takes up whatever position it thinks fit and shells whatever portion of defences or town it feels inclined to. One advantage in a long dragging performance like this is that neither side seems in any particular hurry and a very wet day generally means a certain immunity from fire. Yesterday we had a heavy thunderstorm, and the first flash of lightening exploded one of our mines in front of the brickfields simultaneously with the thunderclap. I felt the ground shake and thought it was a particularly heavy clap of thunder. The mine which was charged with ten pounds of captured nitro-glycerine blew a tremendous hole in the ground, and was, generally speaking, a great success, so what would have happened had their carefully prepared two hundred and fifty pound mine gone off, or what would have been left of Mafeking, I do not like to think. The mine is now recharged and repaired, but I am afraid the Boers have a nasty suspicious disposition which will prevent them from sampling it.

The Cadet Corps have been lately doing their messages mounted on donkeys captured from the Boers. Like the other mounted corps, however, their ranks are gradually being depleted for the soup kitchen. This corps is formed of all the boys of Mafeking, ranging from nine years upwards. It does all the foot orderly work, thereby sparing several more men for the trenches, and is dressed in khaki with "smasher" hats and a yellow puggarree. It is commanded by a youth, Sergeant-Major Goodyear, the son of Captain Goodyear, who was wounded in the brickfields, and is directly supervised by Lord Edward Cecil. It drills regularly, and the boys are wonderfully smart.

Our acetylene search lights on the principle of the duplex heliograph repeat the signals from a central station to the stations all round the outposts, and answer very well. These and all the signalling arrangements are under the charge of Sergeant-Major Moffatt, late Carbineers, who has been very successful on several occasions in tapping the Boers' helio messages. He has also invented a new acetylene signalling lamp, which he has patented, and which he claims can be worked (instead of the helio) on a cloudy day

as well as at night. From what I have seen
of the lamp I think his claims are well
founded.

18th, Wednesday. Desultory shelling.
Last night eleven native women tried to get
out, nine were killed and two were wounded.
This, in spite of repeated protests of Colonel
Baden-Powell, who has pointed out that
Snyman continually shells the native village,
and that when the women try to escape they
are flogged by day and shot by night. Botha,
on hearing of the occurrence, expressed his
great regret and promised to look after the
wounded. Last night, too, the Boers were
blowing up the line to the south, about five
miles out.

19th, Thursday. The Boers are continually
blowing up the line southward, and great
activity prevails around all the laagers, more
particularly at McMullins's. Straws show
which way the wind blows, and we hope this
renewed liveliness portends the approach of
relief. A quiet day. The recent heavy rains
have caused a lot of fever here, but in spite of
that the health of the garrison is on the whole
good.

20th, Friday. Runners arrived with papers and a letter giving an account of the murder of young Dennison at Vryburg. He, it appears, was wounded, and the Boers shot him in cold blood. In the same papers we read accounts of the excellent treatment received by Cronje and the other Boer prisoners, and the infamous treatment accorded to Colonial prisoners of war by the Boers. Having contravened every known law of war, except perhaps poisoning wells, it would seem only reasonable that they should be treated judicially, as they claim to be a civilized race, and given a chance of explaining their breaches of the Geneva Convention. Failing to do this they should be accorded the justice for which they are always clamouring. It appears to me less important to conciliate the rebel Dutch than to avoid stirring up the indignation which is expressing itself very freely amongst the loyal Colonials at the ridiculously lenient way in which the rebels are treated, and as the Bond Attorney-General cannot see his way to proceed against them, it would surely be possible to replace him by an official who was not an avowed sympathiser of theirs. The rebels, so far, apparently have had really a very good time of it. They have looted their loyal neighbours' property, and harried their cattle and farms, murdering them, when so inclined, to their hearts' content, and now are apparently neither going to be asked to pay for their amusement or even disgorge their plunder. You do not as a rule expect the conquered to be satisfied with the victor's settlement of a war, but apparently in our case we are going to pacify our enemies at the expense of our friends. However, I suppose the matter will square itself, and the Colonial troops will not trouble to take prisoners to undergo a farce of a trial.

21st, Saturday. Lord Roberts's message was received yesterday, stating that owing to unforeseen delays the relief column would not be able to reach us by May 18th as originally promised, and asking us to husband our provisions beyond that date. The news had no depressing effect on the town or garrison, and everybody is resolved to undergo anything sooner than surrender. As regards the healthy portion of the garrison the task is a fairly easy one, but for the sick (which are daily increasing in number), the women and children, and the native population to subsist on gradually decreasing rations is indeed hard. Luxuries are, of course, a thing of the past, and it is only with the utmost economy of the necessities of life that our supplies will be equal to the task. However, by the time you get this, the matter will be settled one way or another, but as long as the Union Jack is still flying, any privations will be cheerfully welcomed. The rations now are a quarter-pound of bread, half-pound of meat, supplemented with horseflesh and " sowen " porridge. It is due to the care of the author-ities, and mostly so to Captain Ryan, A.S.C., whose skilful, painstaking, and unwearied manipulation of supplies in the way of calculation, storage, development, and their issue, that we are able even now to live in comparative comfort. He has organised his butcheries and bakeries most admirably. I went round the stores the other day, and paid a visit to his sieving-room, where he has constructed large sieves to sift the fine oatmeal for bread purposes from the husks which are used for making " sowen " porridge, (one hundred pounds of oats producing twenty pounds of fine meal). There I found a dozen or so coal-black individuals under the superintendence of an Englishman, sifting whilst grinning through their covering of flour, and constituting an interesting and very comical spectacle. There is nothing wasted. We eat the fine meal and the "sowen" porridge, the horses eat the refuse from the "sowen" porridge, while we again eat the horses. As a local poet remarks—

"Till the Queen shall have her own again, for the flag we have always flown,
If we cannot live on the fat of the land, we'll fight on the horse and 'sowen.'"

To-day Mrs. Winter and her little boy, aged six, walked to the edge of the town, where recently it has been quiet, but the sight of a petticoat in fancied security was too much for the Boers, for they immediately sniped at her, fortunately, however, without effect.

They were shelling the brickfields to-day, but were otherwise quiet. They, however, nearly hit Colonel Baden-Powell with a shell when he was in that quarter.

22nd, Sunday. A quiet day. The concert in the afternoon was a great success, and Colonel Baden-Powell as usual "brought down the house" in his musical sketches. On reading some old papers I see the Boers have the consummate impudence to protest against our conduct of the war. Now I wish clearly to point out that I do not try to saddle the whole Boer nation with the conduct of some of their worst characters, but the lower class Boer is, in many cases, no better than a savage and sometimes, in the case of educated Kaffirs, considerably worse. I am not trying to pile up atrocities against them, but *à propos* of the subject generally, the following facts are somewhat interesting. George Umfazwi, the head Fingoe, a Christian, is a leading member of the Rev. W. H. Weekes's congregation in the native location. One night he went out cattle-raiding, in charge of a mixed party of Fingoes and Baralongs. These parties, as I have said before, go out on their own initiative, and sell their plunder to the Government. Soon after starting they came upon the body of a Baralong woman, who, when endeavouring to escape, had had

15

her throat cut. Naturally the Baralongs were more than annoyed, and vowed to kill all the Dutch women they might come across. Umfazwi, however, told them that if they persisted in their intentions he and the Fingoes would have nothing more to do with them. In the course of their raid they occupied a Dutch homestead, from which they were fired upon by Dutchmen. In the house were three Dutch women, whom the natives did not touch, only taking the cattle and returning to Mafeking. In the next raid, Umfazwi and his Fingoes were surrounded, as I told you in a former account, and, after a hard fight, were all killed—no quarter being given. I was talking yesterday to Major Anderson, R.A.M.C., and he said, in the course of the conversation, that he preferred a savage warfare, for then you knew what to expect, and that if he had to go out again, he would sooner not take a Red Cross flag, as on each occasion on which he had done so, it had drawn the fire; whereas, when he went out without, he only took his chance with the rest.

23rd, Monday. To-day they shelled the town, doing no damage. They employed a new sort of nine-pounder shell, which will make a nice lamp stand. Two deaths from fever last night, and I fear there will be another death to-day. These late rains have brought out a sort of typhoid malaria.

A most interesting account, from a private soldier's point of view, has been contributed by Private G. Hyslop, Bechuanaland Rifles, to *The Glasgow Weekly Herald*, and though his sources of accurate information are naturally somewhat limited, it is a most fair and intelligent account of the siege.

24th, Tuesday. We received glorious news last night, but it seems almost too good to be true, namely, that Lord Roberts had surrounded the Boers at Kronstadt, and had given them twenty-four hours to surrender, and that Lord Methuen had reached Klerksdorp. It is quite possible, but still one does not like to believe it before it is verified, and it is after all a rumour. On the face of it, it seems probable, and that it is a continuation of his turning movement. If so, the Boers in these parts are nicely out-manœuvred, and we look for our Relief Column following Methuen's tract as far as Border Siding, and

15 *

then coming up the line. Automatic relief, so glibly talked about in some papers, will not be of much use to us, for what we most require is provisions. I saw it stated in an article in *The Times* that Kimberley and ourselves were of no strategical importance in the campaign, but I totally disagree with this idea. Had Mafeking and Kimberley fallen at first, or had Cronje been able to disregard these two isolated places and swept down south, the Colony, to a great extent, would have fallen into his hands. The troops in the South would have had a far greater extent of country to reconquer, and Mafeking at any rate must have eventually fallen. The natives would have lost confidence, the Boers would have retained possession of the line and the rolling stock from the Vaal River to the north, Rhodesia would have been open to attack, and the whole conditions of the war entirely changed, and not changed in our favour. I suppose this also holds good of Ladysmith, but there, of course, the Boers would have left a considerable force in their rear. I think it was the half-heartedness of the Boers in only partially invading

the Colony and Natal and remaining to nibble
at the tempting baits of apparently two
unprotected towns, which gave the troops
coming out an advantage which they never
would have had had the Boers made one
dash for Capetown. And even now, though
in a very much less degree, I consider
this town of strategical importance. We
keep a large number of Boers in our
proximity, and the Boers in the neighbouring
districts are more concerned about preventing
our relief than in opposing the force from
which the really imminent danger threatens.
And if it be true that Lord Methuen is at
Klerksdorp, the Boers in these parts will
have no earthly weight in the decisive portion
of the campaign. Why they should wish to
take Mafeking except to score one trick, as
all other advantages they have gained they
have since lost, it is hard to say. Their
chance of invading Rhodesia is gone, the
crossings of the Vaal River are in our hands.
There are no stores now in Mafeking and
beyond the bare temporary possession, they
would gain nothing at all, added to which
I should have thought that by this time they

might have learnt that they were not going to have even a temporary possession.

The verdict of the court martial which tried Lieutenant Murchison for the murder of Mr. Parslow and sentenced him to death, has come back confirmed by Lord Roberts, who, however, has commuted the sentence to one of penal servitude for life. Murchison was at one time a major in the Royal Artillery, and so far as I know him personally, I do not consider him responsible for his actions.

The Rhodesian postal authorities notified us to-day that press telegrams (owing to the congestion of the lines) would be taken off the wires at Umtali, sent by train to Beira, and then be re-telegraphed to London *viâ* Lorenzo Marques. The press has naturally protested strongly, as their course of action will probably entail a delay of a week. The postal arrangements throughout the campaign have been most infamous ; whether the fault lies at Cape Town or Bulawayo I know not, but in any case some abominably careless official should be hauled over the coals. We have consistently got letters out from here which have been received at home, and it simply means total imbecility or inexcusable idleness on the part of responsible authorities if we are unable to receive letters in the same way. Most people here naturally say it is the fault of the Bond Government, and though they have deserved hanging many times over, I do not think this particular crime can be laid at their door, though the absence of our guns certainly may. Mr. Schreiner has, I see, protested against the Boers being sent to St. Helena. I am unaware if he has protested against our being detained here. He also states that people misjudge him and he seems annoyed. He has only been judged by his actions, which here, as well as elsewhere, are deplored. However, this savours of politics, and is therefore somewhat out of my province.

25th, Wednesday. Last night we received warning from native sources that the Boers intended to make an attack on the town to-day, and that it was to be a personally conducted tour by young Eloff, who had been sent from Pretoria to take Mafeking or die in the attempt. He is, or ought to be, very much alive, for his operations were conducted from a safe distance and the town is much as usual. Of late we have been so dull here, that a considerable amount of fictitious enthusiasm was boiled up over this impending attack. Mr. Hamilton of *The Times* thought it was good enough to sleep in the advanced trench, but the more wary and possibly less enthusiastic, amongst which I include myself, considered a good bed was preferable to an indifferent one. However, I looked out cartridges and laid out weapons when I went to bed, but didn't wake any earlier next morning, and was roused by Ronny Moncreiffe shouting out, "Get up, there is a battle going on." I vainly tried to persuade him to allow me to remain in bed until the enemy were near enough to be dangerous, but he insisted that I should get up and look on. I decided there was no immediate necessity for weapons, and rode off to the nearest telescope to find the enemy. At the B. S. A. P. fort I found the officers of the Protectorate Regiment just coming off the roof, yawning and looking very bored. They told me what had happened up till my arrival, and I went

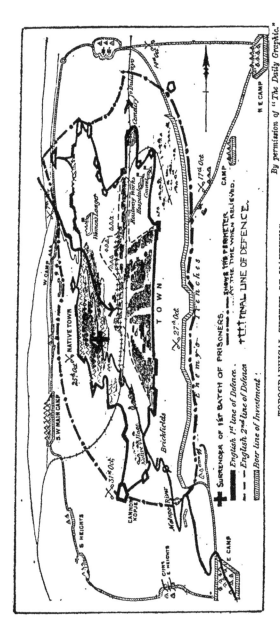

TOPOGRAPHICAL SKETCH OF MAFEKING.

By permission of "The Daily Graphic."

and looked through the telescope for a bit
at our friends the enemy whom we could
clearly see. They were firing their guns
and maintaining a heavy musketry fire,
though in somewhat purposeless manner
about one thousand five hundred yards
from our advanced trench. A gentleman
on horseback, presumably the dashing
Eloff, galloped out from the western
laager, and with many gesticulations and
fruitless haranguing endeavoured to get them
to advance, but they were obdurate. They
pitched one or two shells up by the fort,
which were promptly annexed by piccaninnies,
as the majority did not burst, and they killed
a nigger, and a ricochet hit old Whitfield in the
stomach, but, owing to the width of his figure,
the bullet did not penetrate. I think what
put them off most was our absolute silence.
We did not fire at all except some twenty
rounds at some Boers that had been ambushed
in the culvert, which had the effect of driving
them into some bushes, where they hid
for a couple of hours. I really think the
people surrounding us here have honestly
had enough of it, and it will take a better

man than young Eloff to bring them up to
the scratch, though there are certainly more
Boers about here than there have been for
some time. The object of this particular
attack was to draw our fire and make us
disclose our positions on the western front,
and the result was a most conspicuous failure.
We refused to be drawn by the feint, and so
the real attack, which was supposed to be
concealed elsewhere, was never able to
develop. Apparently the plan was good, like
General Trochu's, but it has at any rate so
tired them that they have been unable to do
anything since.

26th, Thursday. Received my first letters
since this abominable isolation commenced.
One from Weston-Jarvis and another from
Smitheman. Weston is very cheerful.
Smitheman, extravagant as regards paper,
and rather sparing of words and ink ; I also
received some *Morning Posts*, and see that
I have successfully established communication,
which is satisfactory.

27th, Friday. More runners, but thanks
to the usual breakdown of the Beira-Salisbury
line, dates and news are so mixed, and the

contending forces seem so extraordinarily and intricately involved with each other, that we have given up trying to understand how things really are going. It doesn't very much matter, as the result is a foregone conclusion, and at the worst can only be shortly delayed. One thing is amusing, and that is to see the various reasons different countries give for not offering to mediate.

28th, Saturday. Nothing doing. Preparing for the tournament to-morrow. My Kaffir wishes to go and join Plumer. He doesn't approve of the food supply of Mafeking. I thought I should never get rid of him. Thank goodness the brute has gone now. He has been a sort of " old man of the sea " to me. I only kept him because he appeared generally in small health, but when he flung his rations into the middle of the square yesterday, I thought it was high time for him to be off. The last few days the enemy has been more busy on the northeastern front, and established themselves in a sniping trench seven hundred yards from our advanced trench, and made themselves rather a nuisance. We, however, made it so warm

for them that they are concluded to have
withdrawn, but everywhere else, since the
25th, they have been fairly quiet.

29th, Sunday. A most successful tournament, and almost up to Agricultural Hall
form. Most regiments in the service represented, and the sword mounted and bayonet
dismounted both particularly good. It was
trying work judging on half rations, but well
worth it to see such good sport.

What a funny little Frenchman that Prince
Henri d'Orleans must be ? His compliments to
a French comic paper on caricatures of the
English would almost entitle him to a
prominent position on its staff, where, at any
rate, he would score a greater success than
posing as an unemployed patriot. By the bye,
was he not once attached to the British Army,
and if so, whence this venom ? But of tea-
table tacticians and sofa strategists you must,
indeed, have more than enough. Reading the
papers from home one sees excellent persons
with presumably nothing to do, recommending
people generally to turn the other cheek to the
smiter; personally, I and, indeed, most of my
neighbours, think that the smiter has had

quite sufficient chances at our entire carcasses during the last few months, and if they feel themselves so imbued with an overflowing Christian spirit, I should suggest their taking a turn themselves. I do not love the Boer, and I don't think I shall until the Boer loves me. There is only one way to obtain his respect and even toleration, and that is by proving yourself the better man. There will then be peace in the country which, at the present moment, there is not. I do think, too, that people at home should not be so free in their comments upon intelligence from this part of the world. For many years I have read Mr. Baillie Grohmann's letters on big game shooting with much interest. I have also tried to shoot big game and Boers with about equally moderate success. I do assert most emphatically that the Boers use explosive bullets. I have seen the bullets, heard the bullets, and picked up the base of bullets with fulminate caps in them. They were not Mauser bullets, they were not expanding bullets, they were explosive bullets pure and simple, and the Boers have confessed to their use. Therefore, I think it would only have been

fair had Mr. Baillie Grohmann waited to
know on what grounds people out here have
made these assertions, before writing a somewhat conclusive letter in which the main point
appeared to be that there was no such thing
as an explosive Mauser bullet. It is rather
hard on some hundreds of thousands of
Englishmen who happen to be serving their
country out here, that because they are on
that service they should be immediately considered to be destitute of that sense of fair
play with which the race generally is credited,
and I am sure that Mr. Baillie Grohmann
himself, would be the first to admit it. We
don't expect much more from a Boer than
a bullet, and as far as we know have not
particularly grumbled at their using explosive ones, but it is hard lines to be told
they didn't when we mention the fact.
I personally felt a sense of great disappoint-
ment that I was not reading Mr. Baillie
Grohmann's usual letters to *The Field*, instead
of this one in *The Morning Post*.

We are threatened with another attack
to-morrow. I hope it will be more productive
of bloodshed than the last, because we can

then clear them off a bit, and I hate feeling hungry, as do most of us.

Colonel Baden-Powell has just received a missive from young Eloff, in which he states that he sees in a *Bulawayo Chronicle* that we have concerts, balls, tournaments, and cricket matches on Sundays, and it will be very agreeable to his men to come in and participate as they find it dull outside. Colonel Baden-Powell has answered that he thinks perhaps the return match should be postponed until we have finished the present one and that as we are now two hundred not out, and Snyman, Cronje, &c., have not been successful he would suggest a further change of bowling. With such mild japes we pass the time away, but we shot a Dutchman this morning all the same. A bad joke in these times is worth more than a good pint of porridge, as the former will go round whereas the latter will certainly not. It is very edifying work trying to get fat on laughter and sleep, but hunger is not a very amusing form of entertainment. They have recently manufactured brawn of horse hide. It doesn't sound very appetising but the stock dis-

16

appeared with marvellous rapidity. One
cannot help thinking that after all even
though we be hungry out here, yet we have
the glamour of war over us, whereas at home
in the Metropolis one knows hundreds of men
are worse off than ourselves. It is to be
hoped that our impotent sympathisers will
feed the people they can reach, who, after all,
want it just as much as we do.

30th, Monday. Very tired and stiff after
the tournament. I feel as if all the com-
petitors had been beating me with big sticks.
Talking of sticks and Doctor Leyds, which
always seem associated in my mind, I bought
half a dozen very nice ones yesterday.
I hope Dr. Leyds is having a good time now.
I fancy he will have a moderate one when the
war is over, as most people directly blame
him for any discomforts they may have
undergone. It is only natural for a Dutchman
to fight, but for the man who pulls the
strings and risks other people's skins with
the utmost heroism seven thousand miles off,
you do not feel a great amount of affection
or respect, more particularly when he is living
on the fat of the land and you are rather

hungry. Besides, the fellow is an infernal thief; he has battened on these unfortunate peasants for many years, and at the first pinch of fighting flies and leaves them. I have no use for a creature like that. I was rather amused to hear Sergeant Cooke, of the Bechuanaland Rifles, report having slain a Dutchman this morning. He wasn't in the least elated, and in a shamefaced sort of way said he was afraid it wasn't a sporting shot. He couldn't have been more upset if he had shot a hen pheasant sitting, but to anyone else the episode was distinctly amusing.

1st May, Tuesday. We expect a mail to-day, and this dashing fellow Eloff promised us another attack. He has made it. It was the usual sort of performance, and they blazed away for two or three hours and didn't hit anybody. I got up and looked on, because I felt I ought to, but I was rather cross and very bored. If the fools want to fight, why don't they do it? They are doing themselves no good, and not attaining any object whatsoever. Colonel Baden-Powell told them some months ago they would not take Mafeking " by sitting and looking at the place," but even

16 *

now, if they would sacrifice two or three thousand men, they might get in, but I am afraid they will never try. They make me quite angry, they are so stupid. Here they are, daily losing one or two men, and the greatest success they can show is a few stolen cows, whereas if they would come on and fight properly they wouldn't lose very many more men than they have already, and we should have a chance of a show. Seriously speaking though, it is their duty to take this place, and it is very disheartening waiting for them to try to. We got our pigeon mails to-day; unfortunately, no news whatsoever. We have not received any decisive news or had any optimistic rumour confirmed for weeks, and in fact our last good news is Cronje's mop up. Isn't there an old figure in some square dance or other called the *chassez croissée?* It seems to be fashionable out here. I don't like square dances or slow generals. As I telegraphed to you this morning my general sensation is that of an aching void. The only satisfaction I can derive therefrom is the certainty that most of my friends and acquaintances will be much amused

at my being kept quiet anywhere on short
commons.   Tom Greenfield is looking terribly
hungry, but then with his length he naturally
takes more filling up than ordinary mortals.
Godley, too, looks as if he could do with a bit
more, but he always is thin.   We have got
a very tall lot of men here, Cecil, Tom Greenfield, Godley, Fitzclarence, Bentinck, all make
an ordinary six-foot individual feel small, and
McKenna isn't exactly short.   If we have
length represented we also have breadth,
which even our present rations are unable to
reduce.   I am certainly not going to quote
a nominal roll of these individuals, as they
are fine strong men and I can't get away.

2nd, Wednesday.   This morning firing is
going on.   I suppose another attack.   I will
go out and see.   One rather funny incident
in connection with the Boer attack took place
yesterday.   As a rule they knock off for breakfast, but yesterday they kept it up till some
time past 8 o'clock, so at 8 o'clock punctually
the natives left their trenches with their
tins to draw their porridge, absolutely disre-
garding the Boer fire which was renewed at
intervals all day.   It is perfectly incredible

how we have pushed them back, for within the area where our advanced trenches now are I recollect seeing a horse-battery of theirs in action during the first few days of the siege. They take particular care not to play those games now. I only wish they would. This sort of drivel relieves one's feelings, even if one can't see relief.

3rd, Thursday. Firing yesterday and to-day was not of any value ; they kept it up off and on all day. I sat on the roof with the officers of the Bechuanaland Rifles, and looked on till we got bored. The operation of getting on to and off the roof again was far more dangerous than the ordinary Boer battle. This evening I rode round the guards with Major Panzera. It would take a more enterprising Boer than we have run up against to get in. Major Panzera has a theory that he can't be hit; I haven't, however. Both our theories are good enough viewed from the light of experience.

The Germans participating in the defence of the town are going to be photographed. I feel sorry for the German Emperor not being here. He would enjoy this war thoroughly.

I heard from Weston-Jarvis this morning.
He wrote a very cheery letter. At last they
appear to be making some effort to relieve us.
Why on earth they didn't try before, Heaven
only knows ! It seems a perfectly simple
operation for any man of any ordinary sense,
but really it doesn't much matter in the long
run whether it is a month or two sooner or
later. I also see the "Baron" is coming
down to relieve us. I hope he won't fall on
his head and get stretched out as he usually
persists in doing. We are always meeting
each other in some old ship or other, or in
some out of the way continent, but certainly
I never expected to be relieved by the
"Baron" in the middle of Africa; however,
the more pals that roll up the better.

4th, Friday. Absolute quiet. My last
letters have fallen into the Dutchmen's hands.
They will be nice light reading for them, as
they were barely complimentary. I do not
expect to be popular after this war. When
one is tired and bored out here, it is very
refreshing to be able to abuse all and sundry,
and think that one need not settle up for
another two or three months.

5th, Saturday. Life is short, but temper is shorter. Runners in but no news. This morning a funeral party of the Bechuanaland Rifles marched from the hospital to the cemetery to bury the remains, I say advisedly remains, of Lance-Corporal Ironside, who, after having been wounded some two months ago, had recently had his leg amputated, and had at last died from sheer weakness. He bore his extreme sufferings with remarkable fortitude, pluck, and cheeriness. He was a Scotchman, from Aberdeen, and one of the best shots in the garrison. It is satisfactory to think that he had already avenged his death before he was wounded.

6th, Sunday. To-day the Boers most deliberately violated the tacit Sunday truce which, at their own instigation and request, we have always observed. The whole proceedings were very peculiar. It was a fine morning, and the Sabbath calm pervading the town and the surrounding forts was manifest in the way we were all strolling about the market square. As regards myself, I had just purchased some bases of shells at Platnauer's auction mart, where the weekly auction was proceeding. The firing began, and nobody paid much attention except the officers and men belonging to the quarter at which it was apparently directed. They, on foot, horseback, and bicycle, dispersed headlong to their various posts. One, Mr. McKenzie, on a bicycle, striking the railway line, reached his post in four minutes and fifteen seconds, fifteen seconds too quick for the Boer he was enabled to bag. The Boers, who on previous Sundays had displayed an inclination to loot our cattle, had crept up to the dead ground east of Cannon Kopje, and hastily shot one of our cattle guard and stolen the horses and mules under his charge. It was the more annoying that they should have been successful as we were well prepared for them, and had rather anticipated this attack, having a Maxim in ambush within one hundred and fifty yards, which unfortunately jammed, and failed to polish off the lot, as it certainly ought to have done. If we had had any luck it would have been a very different story. Directly the Maxim began the Boers nipped off their horses and running alongside of them for protection reached the cover in the fold of the ground. Unfortunately they killed poor Francis of the B. S. A. P. (the second brother who has fallen here since the fighting began) and took all the horses. It was very annoying, but a smart bit of work and I congratulate the Dutchmen, whoever they may be, who conducted it. Still it was a breach of our Sunday truce, and if all is fair in love and war the many irate spectators will have their pound of flesh to ask for later on. It really was a curious sight : lines of men impotently watching the raid and behind them the shouts of the unmoved auctioneer of " Going at fifteen bob." " Last time." " Going." " Going." "Gone," and gone they were undoubtedly, but they were our horses and he was referring to some scrap iron. To cover this nefarious procedure they opened a heavy fire on various outlying forts. We were lucky enough in the interchange of courtesies to secure a Dutchman on the railway line, and as they had practically violated the white flag our advanced posts had great shooting all the afternoon at his friends who came to try to pick him up. We buried Francis this evening. The

concert was put off. A certain amount of
endurance has been shown by the inhabitants and a certain amount of pluck by
the defenders of the town, but prior to
the Boers starting fooling (successful fooling
and neatly carried out), I and several more
were standing in the market square gossiping
about things we did know, and things we
didn't, when we happened to notice a very
weak-looking child, apparently as near death
as any living creature could be. It transpired
on inquiry that this infant was a Dutch one,
Graaf by name. His father, a refugee, died
of fever ; his brother was in hospital, and he
had been offered admission, which he refused,
because he said that he must look after his
mother. Even then, though scarcely able
to cross the road, the kid was going to
draw his rations. He was taken to hospital,
but I think that this is about the pluckiest
individual that has come under my notice,
and nobody can take exception to the child,
though his mother is probably one of those
amiable ladies who eat our rations, betray
our plans, and are always expressing a whole-
hearted wish for our extermination.

15th, Tuesday.   News has arrived that our troops are within striking distance ; " Sister Ann " performance has begun again.   We are now beginning to recover from our exciting Saturday.   As I wired home, it was the best day that I ever saw, and I must now try and describe it.

Just before four o'clock in the morning we were roused by heavy firing.   The garrison turned out and manned the various works. We all turned up, and I went to the headquarters.   Everybody got their horses ready, armed themselves as best they could, and awaited the real attack.   Colonel Baden-Powell said at once the real attack would be on the stadt.   We have had a good many attacks and don't attach much importance to them, but we did not any one of us anticipate the day's work that was in store for us. When I say anticipate, every possible preparation had been made.   Well, we hung about in the cold.   After about an hour and a half the firing on the eastern front began to slacken.   Trooper Waterson of the Blues, as usual, had coffee and cocoa ready at once, and we felt we could last a bit.   Jokes were freely bandied, and we kept saying, " When are they going to begin ? " Suddenly on the west a conflagration was seen, and betting began as to how far out it was. I got on to the roof of a house, and with Mr. Arnold, of Dixon's Hotel, saw a very magnificent sight. Apparently the whole stadt was on fire, and with the sunrise behind us and the stadt in flames in front, the combination of effects was truly magnificent, if not exactly reassuring. However, nobody seemed to mind much. Our guns, followed by the Bechuanaland Rifles, hurried across the square, men laughing and joking and saying, " we were going to have a good fight." Then came the news that the B.S.A.P. fort, garrisoned by the Protectorate Regiment, had fallen into the enemy's hands. Personally I did not believe it to be true, and started with a carbine to assure myself of the fact. I got close up to the fort, met a squadron running obliquely across its front, and though the bullets were coming from that direction could not believe but that they were our own men who were strolling about outside it. That is the worst of being educated under black powder. I saw poor

Hazelrigg, who was a personal friend of mine, and whom I knew at home, shot, but did not realise who he was. Both sides were inextricably mixed, but having ridden about, and got the hang of things, I am certain that within twenty minutes, order and confidence were absolutely restored on our side. You saw bodies of men, individuals, everybody armed with what they could get, guns of any sort, running towards the firing. A smile on every man's face, and the usual remark was, "Now we've got the beggars." The "beggars" in question were under the impression that they had got us and no doubt had a certain amount of ground for their belief. The fight then began. At least we began to fight, for up till then no return had been made to the very heavy fusillade to which we had been subjected. I have soldiered for some years and I have never seen anything smarter or better than the way the Bechuanaland Rifles, our Artillery and the Protectorate Regiment ran down and got between the Boers and their final objective. The Boers then sent a message through the telephone to say they had got Colonel Hore

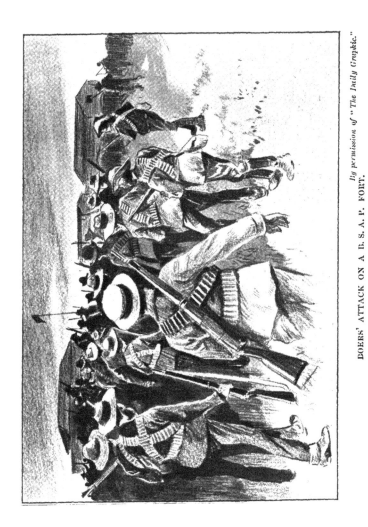

BOERS' ATTACK ON A B. S. A. P. FORT.

and his force prisoners and that we could not touch them. Campbell, our operator, returned a few remarks of his own not perhaps wholly complimentary and the telephone was dis-connected and re-connected with Major Godley. Our main telephone wire runs through the B. S. A. P. fort. McLeod, the man in charge of the wires, commenced careering about armed with a stick and a rifle, and followed by his staff of black men with the idea of directly connecting Major Godley's fort and the headquarters. I may mention McLeod is a sailor and conducts his horse on the principle of a ship. He is perhaps the worst horseman I have ever seen and it says much for the honour of the horse flesh of Mafeking that he is still alive. However, be that as it may, his pawky humour and absolute disregard of danger has made him one of the most amusing features of the siege. You always hear him in broad Scotch and remarkable places, but he is always where he is wanted. By this time we were settling down a bit, so were they. They looted everything they possibly could. A Frenchman got on to the roof of the fort with a bottle of Burgundy belonging to the officers' mess to drink to " Fashoda." He got hit in the stomach and his pals drank the bottle. Our men were very funny. When the Frenchmen yelled " Fashoda," they said " silly beggars, their geography is wrong." I was very pleased with the whole day. I have never heard more or worse jokes made, and, no doubt, had I been umpiring, I should have put some of us out of action or at any rate given them a slight advantage. Every townsman otherwise unoccupied, who had possibly never contemplated the prospect of a fight to the finish, now turned out. Mr. Weil (and too much cannot be said for his resource through every feature of the siege) broke open his boxes, served out every species of firearms he could to every person who wanted them.

A very deaf old soldier, late of the 24th Regiment, Masters by name, asked where they were, and then proceeded to investigate in a most practical fashion. I went down to the jail which more or less commands the B.S.A.P. fort and buildings, and had a look, and

as we saw that no attack was imminent or at
any rate likely to prove successful, we knocked
off by parties and had our breakfast. We
were beginning to kill them very nicely.
Jail prisoners had all been released.
Murchison, who shot Parslow, Lonie, the
greatest criminal of the town, were both armed
and doing their duty. We were all shooting
with the greatest deliberation and effect whenever they showed themselves, and perhaps
I was better pleased with being an Englishman
from a sightseer's point of view than on any
day since the Jubilee. The quaint part of the
whole thing was that we were shooting at
our own people unwittingly. I had a cousin
there, and we laughed consumedly in the
evening when we exchanged notes and
found that we had been shooting close to
him amongst others. I don't think that
any man who was in that fight will ever
think ill of his neighbour from the highest to
the lowest; from our General—or, at least,
he ought to be a General—to the ordinary
civilian, everbody was cheerful and confident
of victory. We had had a long seven
months' wait, and at last we were having our

17

decisive fight. After breakfast (like giants refreshed) we began shooting again. I cannot tell you who did well, but I can assure you that no man did badly. Besides the men there were ladies. Mrs. Buchan and Miss Crawford worked most calmly and bravely under fire. All the other ladies did their duty too. Whilst the fight was developing, Mrs. Winter was running about getting us coffee. Her small son, aged six, was extremely wroth with me because I ordered him under shelter. Then commenced what you may call the next phase of the fight. Captain Fitzclarence and his squadron, with Mr. Swinburne and Mr. Bridges, came down through the town to join hands with Captain Marsh's squadron, and then with Lord Charles Bentinck's squadron and the Baralongs, the whole under Major Godley, were now going to commence to capture the Boers. I must endeavour to describe the situation. Eloff's attack was clever and determined. He had seven hundred men and had advanced up the bed of the Molopo. Into Mafeking he had got, but like many previous attacks had proved—it was easy to get in, but quite another matter to get out. The

BOERS FIRING THE NATIVE STADT.

Baralongs and our outlying forts had allowed
some three hundred men to enter, and had
then commenced a heavy fire upon their
supports. This discomfited the supports,
and they incontinently fled. Silas Moleno
and Lekoko, the Baralong leaders, had
decided that it was better to kraal them
up like cattle. One Dutchman was overheard
to shout, "Mafeking is ours," when suddenly
his friends yelled, "My God, we are surrounded." This species of fighting particularly appeals to the Baralong. He is better
than the Boer at the Boer's own game, and
never will I hear a word against the Baralong.
However, Silas was then engaged in con-
junction with our own men in collecting
them. He collected them where they had
no water, and then the question resolved
itself into the Boer showing himself and
getting shot or gradually starving. If the
Baralongs had been fighting the fight and
time had been no particular object, they would
probably still be shooting odd Boers, but it is
obvious that those dilatory measures could not
be pursued by ourselves, and that we had to
finish the fight by nightfall. Our men were

17 *

accordingly sent down to round them up;
there were thus in all three parties of Boers
in the town, one, nearly three hundred strong,
in the B. S. A. P. fort, sundry in a kraal by
Mr. Minchin's house, others again in the
kopje. The kraal was captured in an
exceedingly clever manner. Captain Fitzclarence and Captain Marsh worked up to the
walls, but knowing the pleasant nature of the
Boer, instead of storming the place or
showing themselves, they bored loopholes
with their bayonets. The artillery under
Lieutenant Daniels also had come up to
within forty yards. There was a slight
hesitation on the part of the Boers to surrender. The order was given to the gun to
commence fire. The lanyard broke, but before
a fresh start could be made the Boers hastily
surrendered. Captain Marsh, known and
respected by the Baralongs, had great difficulty in restraining them from finishing the
fight their own way, and small blame to them
for their desire. They had had their stadt
burned. Odd Boers had been bolting at intervals, and had mostly been accounted for. The
question next to be settled was as to the

possession of the B. S. A. P. fort. Our men
who were captive therein, and indeed the Boers
and foreigners to whom I have since talked
describe our fire as extraordinarily accurate.
Eloff had great difficulty in keeping his
men together, and as one man at least was
a deserter of ours, it can't altogether be
wondered that they did not wish to remain.
Our firing, as we had more men to spare,
became more and more deadly, and at last
now they decided to surrender. Some
hundred broke away and escaped from the
fort, in spite of Eloff firing on them, but
their bodies have been coming in ever since
and many will never be accounted for,
because the bodies of men with rifles may
be possibly put away by the Baralongs,
who are always begging rifles we have been
unable to give them. Eloff accordingly
surrendered to Colonel Hore. The other
party in the kopje had made several unsuccessful attempts to break out, Bentinck and
his squadron always successfully heading
them, but as it got dark, and our men had
been fighting from before four, it was decided
to let them break out and just shoot

what we could. The Baralongs had some
more shooting too. As each successive
batch of prisoners was marched into the
town absolute silence was maintained by
the Britishers, except saluting brave men
who had tried and failed. They were brave
men and I like them better now than I ever
did ; the Kaffirs, however, hooted. As each
batch marched up, their arms, of which
they had naturally been deprived, were
handed over to the Cadets, who had been
under fire all day. These warriors range
from nine to fifteen years of age. They
are the only smartly clad portion of the
garrison, for our victorious troops were
the dirtiest and most vilely robed lot of
scarecrows I have ever seen, still it did
one good to see the escort to the prisoners,
they were simply swelling like turkey cocks
and all round our long lines of defences we
would hear cheers and " Rule Britannia " and
the " Anthem " being sung with the wildest
enthusiasm. It is impossible as I said before, to
say who behaved best, but none behaved badly.
There was only one thing said afterwards, when
all sorts and conditions of men were shaking

CAPTURED BOER PRISONERS.

By permission of "The Daily Graphic."

each other by the hand, and that was, " This is a great day for England." Mafeking is still rather mad with the Relief Column within shouting distance and it is likely to remain so.

We lost few men in our great success but I take it that no man particularly wants to be lost. I really have seen brave men here, but the man who says he wants to get shot is simply a liar. We know the story of the Roman sentinel and the Highlander who fought in Athlone (or was it Mullingar) against Hoche and many men that have died for their country obstinately. Captain Singleton's servant, Trooper Muttershek, may be added to their roll. He absolutely declined to surrender and fought on till killed. It wasn't a case of dashing in and dashing out and having your fun and a fight, it was a case of resolution to die sooner than throw down your arms, the wisdom may be questionable, the heroism undoubted. He wasn't taking any surrender. As far as I am concerned, I have seen the British assert their superiority over foreigners before now, but this man in my opinion, though I didn't see him die, was the bravest man who fought on either

side that day. It is a good thing to be
an Englishman. These foreigners start too
quick and finish quicker. They are good
men, but we are better, and have proved
so for several hundred years. I had always
wanted to see the Englishman fight in a
tight hole, and I know what he is worth
now. He can outstay the other chap. Well,
you must be getting rather bored by the
fighting, and I will write more anon when
I have collected some further particulars.
The Rev. W. H. Weekes, our parson,
organized a thanksgiving service on Sunday
night. We were still rather mad, and it
gave us a pleasant feeling to sing nice
fighting psalms and hymns, because which
ever way you look at it we are perfectly
convinced out here that it is a righteous
war. He had rather a mixed congregation,
which probably in times of peace would be
half the size, but he understands his congregation and the congregation understand him.

Poor Hazelrigg died that night.

I went over and saw the prisoners this
afternoon. They were very civil, and so were
we. I like a Frenchman, and was chaffing

By permission of "The Daily Graphic."

INTERVIEWING BOER PRISONERS ON MR. WEIL'S STOEP.

them more or less at having left "La Patrie."
They didn't seem to mind being prisoners;
they apparently enjoyed their fight, but they
objected to their food. I did what I could for
them, and I couldn't help feeling that they
were absolutely uninvited guests. It wasn't
their quarrel, and why they wanted to shove
their nose into it we all fail to understand.
There is really a very charming man amongst
them, who asked me to procure him a grammar
as he wished to improve his mind by learning
Dutch and English. Of course, I got him
a grammar, while I could'nt help suggesting
that it might have been as well to remain in
comfort in France without travelling all this
way to learn the language, also remarking
Dutch seemed rather out of date. He rather
agreed with me, and asked me for a
collection of siege stamps as he said he
thought his girl would like them. The
funny part of these fellows is that they
seem to think that we haven't got homes or
girls or anything else, but are a sort of
automatic "Aunt Sally," put up here for
irresponsible foreigners to have a shy at.

Nobody bears any malice about the fight, but the Frenchman calls the Boer " canaille," the Boer doesn't seem to like the Frenchman or, indeed, any other foreigner, regarding him as an impetuous fool who would probably lead him (the Boer) into some nasty dangerous place, and the Englishman laughs at the lot; however, as I said before, the poor devils can't help being foreigners. I always like a Frenchman, a good many have been kind to me and they are invariably amusing. Their stomachs, however, are at present proud, and they cannot swallow " sowen," or horse flesh, or any local luxuries. However, as we pointed out, it was rather their fault that we had not any rations in here. Some of these men had only been in the country a week. It seems a long way to come to get put in "quod," and live on horse flesh and " sowens." One told me he passed a battery of our relieving column in harbour at Beira. I suppose he thought he had put in a smart day's work when he got ahead of it. He has, but he isn't working now. I never liked Eloff much, not that I knew him personally, but now I like him

better for his performances. He very nearly
did a big thing, but both sides have apparently
an ineradicable mutual contempt for each
other, which has led to some very pretty fighting
through the whole war. There is no mistake
about it, he did insult the Queen, and I am
glad we have had the wiping out of
that score, but he is a gallant fellow
all the same. When we look back on our
discomfiture of Cronje, and the mopping up
of Eloff, it gives a pleasant finish to the siege.
It wanted just a finishing touch to make it
satisfactory. There should be another fight
within a few hours, but I reckon that it will be
the Relief Column's turn, and though everything is ready for us to assist them I honestly
don't think we could go far and do much. The
men were dog tired on Saturday, absolutely
dog tired. I always thought the Boer was
a bad bird to get up to the gun, but
he came up that day. I don't think he will
again.

On Monday we saw the tail end of some
Boer force arriving. We had hoped it might
be our own people, but they appear to be

a few miles further off. However, we know they are there or thereabouts now. Nobody minds now, we know we are winning.

To return again to my story of the fighting, the foreigners did try their best to stop the Boers looting, but loot they did most thoroughly. They stole everything they could lay their hands on. Not one officer, whose kit happened to be in the fort has recovered anything. One " clumpy " of Boers galloped forth laden with food and drink. The food belonged to themselves, the drink belonged to us. They happened to fall in with the galloping Maxim, a piece of bad luck because they all died and our people took the food and drink. One fellow had taken a pair of brown boots and a horse, he had a few bullets through the boots, the horse was killed and so was he.

Life had been very dull here, but that morning put everything all right. We had never before seen a dead or wounded Boer or a prisoner, and it is weary work to see your friends and neighbours shot and not see your own bag too, but personally, except in the way of business, I hope I haven't killed a Boer. In the fight in the morning, though everything had been prepared for as far as we could tell, we had had to take up positions which were absolutely enfiladed by the fresh development of affairs. The trench occupied by the Bechuanaland Rifles, Protectorate Regiment, and others on the spur of the moment, was directly enfiladed by the enemy's quick-firer. Why we were not wiped out on that line I never shall quite make out. They shot the jailor, Heale, who has done very good work all through the siege, who I am afraid leaves a wife and family. Then the prisoners took charge of themselves. Our gunner prisoners ran down to the guns, one was shot, the others served the gun all day. The others, armed with Martinis, commenced a heavy fire on the enemy, or cautioned the Dutch prisoners, the suspects, as to their behaviour, and put them down a hole. It was an exhilarating sight and struck me as exceedingly quaint to see men who had committed every crime, and were undergoing penal servitude, dismissing their past, oblivious of anything except the fact that we were all of the same crowd, and had got to keep the Dutchmen out.

18

I hope Her Majesty will exercise her clemency; they certainly deserve to regain their rights as citizens.

We have had rather a dull day for some reason or other. A general idea pervaded the town that relief was at hand, and when towards evening a cloud of dust and troops were seen to the south-west, we most of us got on the roofs and looked at them with some interest. It transpired subsequently, however, that they were the enemy retiring before Mahon. They passed round the south of the town, and opposed him later.

16th, Wednesday. A dull day, but towards evening our relief was really seen. Everybody got on the roofs, and looked on at the Boers being shelled; most refreshing, but as they were not apparently coming in, people went to feed, and enthusiasm rather died away again, so much so that when Major Karri Davis, and some eight men of the I. L. I. marched in, he told one passer-by he was the advance guard relief force, the other only murmured "Oh, yes, I heard you were knocking about," and went to draw his rations, or whatever he was busily engaged

in. However, when it became generally
known the crowd assembled and began to
cheer, and go mad again—so to bed.

17th, Thursday. Roused out this morning
at some ungodly hour to be told they had
arrived, and strolled down to the I. L. I. to
see Captain Barnes of my old regiment. It
appeared that Mahon and Plumer had effected
a masterly junction the day before, and that
the former, following the only true policy of
South African warfare had, as usual, said he
was going to do one thing, and done something else, viz., camped out, and then suddenly
inspanned and marched into the town.
I can't quite convey the feelings of the townspeople, they were wild with delight, and
pleased as they were their *bonne bouche*
was to come later. Edwardes and Barnes
breakfasted with me and then went back
(personally I borrowed a horse from the
I. L. I.). About 9 o'clock the guns moved
out to the waterworks, and then the fun
really began. The Boers had been going
to intercept Mahon's entry, but he was a bit
too previous. All the morning their silly
old five-pounder (locally known as "Gentle

18 *

Annie ") had been popping away, when suddenly the R. H. A. Canadian Artillery and pom-poms began, ably led by our old pop-guns, who had the honour of beginning the ball. I rode well out, as I wanted to see the other people have a treat, but literally in half an hour all there was left of the laager, which has vexed our eyes and souls so much for long months, was a cloud of dust on the horizon, except food-stuffs, &c., which we looted. I got a Dutch Bible, and from its tidiness I was pleased to see its late owner was a proficient in the Sunday school. So, quietly back to the town, and after the march past of the relief column the relieved troops began. And now, I suppose, after being bottled up for some eight lunar months, I may effervesce. As I have said before, I have seen many tributes to her Majesty and joined in them all, but dirty men in shirt sleeves, and dirtier men in rags on scarecrows of horses touched me up most of all. We were dirty, we were ragged, but we were most unmistakably loyal, and we came from all parts of the world—Canadians, South Africans, Australians, Englishmen, Indians,

DIXONS. HOTEL

MARCH PAST OF THE RELIEVING FORCE.

By permission of "The Daily Graphic."

and our Cape Boys and various other Africans,
and there was not one of us who did not respect
the other, and know we were for one job, the
Queen and Empire, not one.

I wonder how the prisoners felt, poor devils;
they must have wished they were not against
us. The Boers had certainly executed the
smartest movement I had seen for some time ;
I had not believed it possible that a laager
could break up and disperse so rapidly. We
all went back to lunch, having recovered
Captain McLaren, who, I am glad to say, is
doing very well. Then after lunch an alarm
was raised that we had rounded up old
Snyman, and everybody started off to help
in the operation ; but, alas, Snyman knows
too much. They said that he and four hundred Boers were surrounded and refused to
surrender, and we all wanted as much surrender as we could get—or the other thing.
I am glad to say he was hit on the head in
the morning with a bit of shrapnel, but not
dangerously wounded, unfortunately, at least
so they report. He seems equally execrated
by Dutch and English — Psalm - singing,
sanctimonious murderer of women and

children and his son takes after him. I may contradict my previous statements, but his actions have also varied frequently. Well, we had a great dinner ; old friends from all parts of the world foregathered, and at our head was Smitheman. Many dinners then combined, and more old friends were met—so to bed, still pleased with England. Men of all sorts and conditions, trades, professions and ranks, relievers and relieved, slept that night in and about Mafeking, with a restless sleep, thinking of what England would think, and we knew and were sorry we couldn't hear what they said.

The garrison in Mafeking hope to get some recognition or decoration, but what they attach particular importance to is receiving the Queen's chocolate.

Immediately after the relief column marched in our Baralongs under Montsoia Wessels, Silas and Sekoko and Josiah, marched off on their own to settle up Abraham Ralinti at Rietfontein, and bring in our trusty ally, Saani. He had been utterly looted, and taken away from his own stadt, and kept a prisoner at Rietfontein, his great notion being that we should have a conference with the Boers, and then lay down what he called "plenty polomite," and blow them up when they came to confer. You cannot get very far ahead of a Baralong. I suppose this is the first occasion on which one black man surrendered under a white flag to another. These Rietfontein rebels have always been against the remainder of the Baralongs, and have invariably fought for the Boers since the disturbed relations between Briton and Boer have existed. I hope they will shoot Abraham, as his people's invariable cunning in stopping our runners has caused us great inconvenience, not to mention the numbers they have killed.

18th, Friday. Did very little. Went round and helped our pals to shop, get stamps, money, &c., &c.

19th, Saturday. The garrison held its solemn Thanksgiving Service at the cemetery, at the termination of which three volleys were fired over our dead. We had been unable to do this before owing to the certainty of drawing fire, not that that really much mattered, as they usually fired on all our funeral parties, though there could be no mistaking them. Still they had this excuse that the cemetery is fortified. After the last post had sounded we reformed and sang the National Anthem. Then, after Colonel Baden-Powell had spoken personally to each detachment, we cheered him, and then with heartfelt cheers for Her Majesty, the siege of Mafeking closed.

GOD SAVE THE QUEEN.

And now for sheer personalities. Mr. Stuart had arrived, and as I considered he was much better qualified to represent the paper with the force than myself, I determined to come south. Mr. B. Weil, whom as I have previously said, I consider to be one of the principal factors in the successful defence, certainly as regards the food supply, said he was going south. I accordingly resolved to accompany him, and while returning from the ceremony suggested it. Anyhow, to make a long story short, I arrived as he was starting, and with a small bag, having relinquished all my Mafeking impedimenta, climbed into his cart. He had to turn out one of his boys, but I didn't mind that, and being the most good-natured of men, he tried to look as if he didn't. So our caravan started — Major Anderson, Major Davis (Surg. I. L. I.), Mr. Weil, and myself, together with his servant Mitchell, a prototype of "Binjamin," but absolutely reliable and hard-working, also Bradley, of Bradley's Hotel, Inspector Marsh, the Rev. — Peart, and Ronny Moncrieffe (who had secured a horse belonging to a Protectorate regiment, and proposed to accompany us). He had done a lot of good work in the siege, and was about as tired and unfit as a man could be. However, he was determined to get through, and so he did. It was a quaint pilgrimage, as the column, though it had swept the country, had not particularly cleared it, and the Boer is here to-day, gone to-morrow, and back the next day. Well, our commissariat was excellent. I contributed some eight biscuits and three tins of bully, and that is all I have done except live on the fat of the land—Lord, how fat it seemed after Mafeking—a land flowing with fresh milk, butter and eggs, mutton and white bread, and above all, the sense of freedom. I

never knew what it felt like to be properly
free before, and I have been more or less of
a wanderer most of my life. No more sieges
for me, except perhaps from the outside. Yet
I was sorry to leave Mafeking, and I may
truly say as far as I know I didn't leave a bad
friend behind me, only all my kit. Towards
dark, after an outspan that was like a picnic,
we reached Mr. Wright's farm, where the
wounded were—one had died the night before
—and we found Mr. Hands, *Daily Mail*, badly
wounded in the thigh, but doing well; Captain
Maxwell, I. S. C., and others. Mr. Wright
acts up to his name. Two of his sons were
in "tronk" at Zeerust for refusing to join the
Boers, and what he had was at our disposal.
I wonder if people at home realize in what
a position our loyalists in Bechuanaland have
been placed. If they didn't come in their own
countrymen regarded them as rebels,—if they
did they lost all they had. But by doing as
they have done, that is by carrying on their
business while exposed to all the contumely
and insult the Boers could heap on them, with
the possible loss of life as well as property,
they have served their country as well

as those who have taken up arms; because
their houses have always been a safe place for
runners to go to, and news about the doings
of the Boers could be obtained from them.
Besides, they know which of the Boers
fought, and which didn't, and this fact now
terrifies the rebels and keeps many quiet, who
might not otherwise be so. Mr. Weil on arrival
bought two hundred bags of mealies and
despatched them to his friends the Baralongs.
Such a pretty place his farm is, with plenty
of water and lots of game. We slept under
the cart, and miserably cold it was. Mr. Weil
(who is rather like myself in that respect),
could not sleep, and was determined nobody
else should do so. So we got up, and sat round
the fire till sunrise. Our cocoa that morning
was indeed acceptable. The caravan, which
was as I say, quaint, marched as follows, preceded by mounted Kaffir Scouts:—First came
Keeley and his boy in a Cape cart drawn by
mules, followed by Weil, his servant, driver
and myself in another Cape cart with six
mules, Bradley driving a pair of horses in
another, then Ronny, the Rev. — Peart and
Inspector Marsh riding, the latter riding B. P.'s

brother's pony. We inspanned at sunrise on
Monday and started for Setloguli. Halted
half way and had the pleasing intelligence that
a commando was raiding within six miles of
us. I personally felt very unhappy. I had
always looked upon it as a two-to-one chance,
and as we had no weapons we could make no
fight of it. Apart from the bore of being a
prisoner I knew I should be so awfully laughed
at. However, there we were—it was no use
grumbling, but I did, as hard as ever I could.
Then we inspanned and drove to Setloguli,
where our spirits were considerably raised by
an excellent lunch provided by Mrs. Fraser,
who is the best hostess I have ever met. The
Frasers had a terrible rough time of it, and
now " the Queen had got her own again " were
naturally correspondingly cheerful. Later
we were also further relieved to hear that " the
commando " was merely a small patrol of Boers,
and that it had withdrawn across the border.
During the afternoon I went up and saw the
old fort—quite interesting, and anybody who
wants to spend a quiet time might do worse than
to go to Setloguli. The worst of it is it takes
some time to get there. Lady Sarah Wilson's

maid was there. She had been there since Lady Sarah was brought in by the Boers to Mafeking. Mr. Weil was showing various curios of the siege to Mrs. Fraser, including a copy of Her Majesty's *Leaves from the Journal of our Life in the Highlands*, which he had looted from the Boer laager. This excited the good lady's unqualified wrath, " What sacrilege for them to have it in their hands. Why it smells Boery," she said. On Tuesday Keeley was returning to Mafeking with Lady Sarah's maid and his scouts, so Weil engaged two scouts to accompany us to Jan Modebi, where we were next going to stop. They didn't seem particularly pushing sort of scouts, as they persistently rode in rear of the Cape cart. The road too, was infamous, but it was impossible to lose the way as the column had left an unmistakable track behind them, and this was fortunate, because when we had been going about an hour and a half our intelligent guide stated he didn't know the way. I wonder how Keeley felt all that Tuesday. If he could have heard half we said he would have torn his two days' beard out and wept. The other scout lost us altogether. Keeley and Weil were arranging a series of despatch riders, so as long as we got one of them to Jan Modebi's, it didn't much matter. We outspanned first at a rebel's farm, and had an excellent lunch. I was still rather fretful. The prospect of captivity made me so, and I only believe in dead Dutchmen, till peace is proclaimed.

One Sonnenberg, a brother of some Bond member or other, was there trading, I suppose, like most Bondsmen, running with the hare and hunting with the hounds. He looked well on it, and was very civil. We inspanned and then came a long trek to Jan Modebi's. About half-way there, we saw two horsemen with guns cruising about. One obviously was not a soldier. I reckoned Pretoria was the ticket, however, they came up and Weil went to interview them. They turned out to be one of the Kimberley Light Horse and a civilian who was showing him the way, and he said he had got a convoy of cattle. It felt like being near home again then. We afterwards met the convoy—total, four white men and five black. I still marvel at their colossal impudence, marching through a rebel country within five miles of the enemy's border, escorting cattle for which any Boer will peril his skin. He calmly assured me they were going to pick up all they saw on the way; to use his own words, " All is fish that comes to our net." I hope they got through all right. So to Mr. Menson's, where we put up for the night, and he, like everyone else, did all he could. He, too, had had a bad time. He didn't grumble, but when the relief column had come through they had cut all his barbed wire fences. Having a constitutional antipathy to barbed wire I sympathized with the relief column, but naturally did not say so. I was amused to see three prints of Sir Alfred Milner, Lord Roberts, and Oom Paul, the inscription under the latter being, " The end is better than the beginning, 14.10.99," also to hear his account of how when driving his cattle to Vryburg at the outbreak of the war he had met a Dutchman who told him that they had driven the English into the sea. His reply was, " Oh, that's too far to go," and so he turned and drove his cattle back again to his farm. Weil, as usual, bought up cattle, &c., also butter and other luxuries, and despatched them to the hospital at Mafeking on his own account.

Wednesday. We started rather later than usual owing to the heavy rain, and half way to Vryburg we crossed the fresh spoor of men, wagons, cattle, &c., going towards the Transvaal. It afterwards transpired it was the rebel Van Zyl and his following, bolting from Kuruman to the Transvaal. Let off number two. We couldn't have been more than an hour or two behind them, and they would certainly have scooped us had we met them, so the rain was lucky. Well, we got into Vryburg from one side as the troops got in from the other. An old acquaintance rushed me off to the Club, and I then strolled up to see the Scotch Yeomanry and found Charley Burn, I found also Kidd and several others I knew—then on to see Reade, who had been Intelligence Officer at Mafeking before the war, and was D. A. A. G. to General Barton, and arranged about getting on in the first train. This was my first chance of seeing the infantry Tommy on the war path to any great extent. He is no more beautiful or clean, in fact, if

anything less so than his cavalry brother,
but by heaven he looks a useful one ! However, what matter the man as long as the
flag is clean. Met North of the Royal
Fusiliers and dined with him, they all asked
after Fitzclarence, Godley, and the others.
They and the Scots Fusiliers had done quite
an extraordinary march of forty-four miles in
thirty-four hours, and now our infantry were
within striking distance of Mafeking. The
line should soon be repaired as they had
begun from Mafeking and the line as far as
Maribogo was practically untouched, in fact
next morning, Thursday, they ran twelve
miles north. Thursday we began our preparations for departure. The garrison were
preparing to celebrate the Queen's Birthday,
and the populace to display great enthusiasm,
and the women began to come into town. It
was not a highly polished parade, so far as
I could see. Still, it was rather good to have
it there just then, where the Dutchmen had
been in occupation within ten days. Rifles
were now coming in by the hundred, and the
rebel of a fortnight before became a British
patriot. We drove to the station, and there

met the Scots Fusiliers. I was accosted by
a warrior in large blue goggles, who said
I didn't remember him. I naturally didn't in
the goggles, but it turned out to be Scudamore.
They did the best they could for us, and
then Dick of the Royal Irish Fusiliers
turned up, who had once been my sergeant-
major. I was glad to see him—the old
regiment and squadron seems fairly dotted
all over Africa. Barnes was at Mafeking, three
of us had been through the siege, and I met one
Lambart at Taungs, who had been a corporal
with us, and was a captain in the Kimberley
Mounted Corps, curiously enough all belonging to two squadrons, B and D. Well, we
left Vryburg with a light engine and a truck
full of niggers. We were all sitting on
the tank, in charge of young Gregg,
R.E., who is a good train master. He
ran us down, after dropping the niggers
to repair a bridge, to Dry Hartz, where
we had to pull out for an up-coming train,
and as we had half an hour to wait, and it was
just mid-day at twelve, we formed up and gave
three cheers for the Queen and drank her
health. It was the smallest and dirtiest

Queen's Birthday parade I have ever attended; nine all told, but "mony a little makes a muckle." We ran down to Taungs, where one way and another we were detained some twelve hours. I didn't mind. The Royal Welsh Fusiliers were there, and I found several old friends and acquaintances—Gough Radcliffe, R.H., Cooper (Royal Fusiliers), Broke Wright, R.E., the former railway staff officer. So into a cattle truck we jumped with one of the Welsh Fusiliers and some men and arrived at Kimberley 7 o'clock next morning, where I called on Sir C. Parsons, and had fish for breakfast at the hotel. Thus my journey was practically ended. It transpired that Vryburg was held by some half dozen of our forces, and that the remainder of the garrison was only sixty loyalists from the town population. It did not seem a large garrison, but apparently it was good enough. There was rather a curious coincidence at dinner at Orange River. I saw a man whose face I thought I knew, but I was mistaken; it was his likeness to his brother which misled me. He turned out to be Tom Greenfield's brother, who was down here sick, and to whom I had wired to meet me at Fourteen Streams, so that I could give him news of Tom. However, I struck him on the next river or so, so it didn't much matter.

It was sad to pass the Modder River and see our cemeteries—all English; so we passed on to Cape Town. And how jolly it was to see old friends; besides, we were able to tell our Mafeking people, womenfolk, good news of their husbands.

Three pleasant days there, and then everybody came to see us off by the *Norman*, which we nearly missed. The voyage passed without much incident. Everybody on board was more or less personally interested in the war, and there were a good many Boers and pro-Boers on board. On Saturday, short of Madeira, the *Briton* signalled the news of the fall of Pretoria. Tremendous rejoicings on board on the part of the British, while the Dutch were correspondingly depressed and seemed rather sad; some of them wept into the sea.

The further I got from the seat of war the less animus I felt. So to Madeira, where we arrived about midnight, and the news was confirmed with particulars. We got many newspapers. On to Southampton—more victories ; many valuable officers killed. It is really sad to take up a newspaper ; one sees friends killed in every fight. Thus we arrived in London at 9.15 on the 15th June, having left Mafeking 11 a.m. the 20th May.

By permission of " *The Daily Graphic.*"
"LORD NELSON."

By a curious coincidence the letters B. P. were found cast on the breech of this piece when dug up.

By permission of "The Daily Graphic."

Lightning Source UK Ltd.
Milton Keynes UK
UKHW011255011221
394871UK00001B/45

9 781845 747398